Narratives of Human Evolution

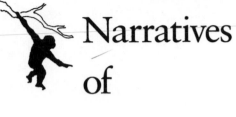

Narratives
of
Human
Evolution

Misia Landau

Yale University Press   New Haven and London

Published with assistance from the foundation established in memory of William McKean Brown.

Library of Congress Cataloging-in-Publication Data

Landau, Misia, 1953–
  Narratives of human evolution /
  Misia Landau.
    p. cm.
  Includes bibliographical references and index.
  ISBN 0-300-04940-4 (alk. paper)
  1. Human evolution.
  2. Anthropology, Prehistoric.
  I. Title.
  GN281.L354 1991
  573.2—dc20   90–45177
                                     CIP

Designed by James J. Johnson.
Set in Sabon types by
Marathon Typography Service, Inc.,
Research Triangle Park,
North Carolina.
Printed in the United States of America.

The paper in this book meets the guidelines for permanence and durability of the Committee on Production Guidelines for Book Longevity of the Council on Library Resources.

10   9   8   7   6   5   4   3   2   1

To my parents,
Madeline and Victor

Contents

Preface

I myself believe that all the magnificent achievements of mathematical and physical science—our doctrines of evolution, of uniformity of law, and the rest—proceed from our indomitable desire to cast the world into a more rational shape in our minds than the crude order of our experience. . . . The principle of causality, for example,—what is it but a postulate, an empty name covering simply a demand that the sequence of events shall some day manifest a deeper kind of belonging of one thing with another than the mere arbitrary juxtaposition which now phenomenally appears? It is as much an altar to an unknown god as the one that Saint Paul found at Athens. All our scientific and philosophic ideals are *altars to unknown gods.*

—WILLIAM JAMES (1897)

Any account of a sequence of events—so that it manifests "a deeper kind of belonging"—is a form of narrative. Even physics addresses questions of the form "how come . . . ?" by presenting repeatable sequences of events whose description and relation must obey stringent (though not necessarily unchanging) criteria of causal "belonging."

There is a group of sciences committed to narrative in a more discursive style than physics and on a different time scale. They seek to reconstruct sequences of events in the past—sequences presumed to be unique or so hugely cyclic that they are beyond experiment. Cosmology and geology are such sciences. Paleontology, or the study of the origin of living things on earth, and paleoanthropology, the study of human evolution, are further examples, in descending order of taxonomic scope and of time scale. Ideally, they should all fit together in a coherent epic account of our world: how it came to be and how humankind came to have its particular place in it.

This book is concerned with the most intimate of the narrative sciences, paleoanthropology. It addresses a group of classic texts in paleoanthropology beginning in the generation of Charles Darwin. It asks what happens if we look at these texts *as* narratives, leaving aside issues of truth or justification. What it finds is that these texts are determined as much by traditional narrative frameworks as by material evidence.

I suggest that all these paleoanthropological narratives approximate the structure of a hero tale, along the lines proposed by Vladimir Propp in his classic *Morphology of the Folktale* (1928). They feature a humble hero who departs on a journey, receives essential equipment from a helper or donor figure, goes through tests and transformations, and finally arrives at a higher state. But it is part of my argument that, as in Propp's tales, this narrative schema can accommodate widely varying sequences of events, heroes and donors corresponding to the underlying evolutionary beliefs of their authors. A main goal of this book is to show how widely the followers of Charles Darwin depart from Darwinian natural selection as the guiding force that helps the hero forward, and how their interpretations of the fossil record vary according to their convictions about this primary causal agent.

My argument, then, has two complementary parts: theories of human evolution are similar in narrative form and, at the same time, very different in meaning. In the Prologue, I present this similarity of narrative form—this altar housing a deep diversity of faiths—and indicate how it may be used as a framework for interpreting theoretical differences, in particular, differences in belief about the causal agent or prime mover in human evolution. These interpretations are presented in the body of the book. Part I introduces the accounts of the nineteenth-century biologists Thomas Henry Huxley and Ernst Haeckel and shows how they paved the way for Darwin's theory of human evolution by natural selection, which is then presented. Part II examines the theories of Arthur Keith and Grafton Elliot Smith, two early twentieth-century paleoanthropologists, and shows how orthogenetic principles assume the donor role, though in very different guises. The theoretical differences between Keith and Elliot Smith were so great as to overshadow the famous Piltdown debate, in which these two men were main antagonists. Part III shows how the "Modern Synthesis" between genetics and evolutionary theory re-established natural selection as the primary creative force, but with certain limitations of power. Even the neo-Darwinians invoke non-Darwinian, and nonmaterialistic, principles when explaining the later stages of human evolution.

As a paleoanthropologist by allegiance and training, I do not pretend to stand outside the narrative practice I examine. It was my familiarity with theories of human evolution that first led me to see the relevance of Propp's method. There have been many developments in the field of literary criticism since Propp wrote his famous book, some of which may be fruitfully applied to paleoanthropological writing (Landau 1981, 1986, 1987). For the present work, I found that Propp's method was the best tool for demonstrating the existence of a basic story line and also for exploring the various causal agents (or donors) in early twentieth-century theories of human evolution. Literary scholars would probably approach these same texts in a different way. For example, they might look for contradictions between the underlying narrative form and its manifest versions. I am less concerned here with how paleoanthropological theories deviate from the underlying narrative form and more with how they deviate from each other.

At times, my argument may appear to place a strain on the Proppian form. It may seem that the Proppian functions are treated as though they were the "real facts" of paleoanthropology. Though it has been my aim to delineate a set of intuitions or expectations which can be confirmed by other paleoanthropologists, and by those who are familiar with these texts, it is also true that these functions are part of a working hypothesis which is as ideological in effect as the narratives I am describing.

This brings me to my reasons for undertaking this work. It is my belief that scientists have much to gain from an awareness that they are storytellers. My purpose is not to reduce theories of human evolution to formulaic old wives' tales but instead to open them up to new narrative formulations. In the Epilogue, I discuss how an understanding of narrative can provide tools for creating new scientific theories as well as for analyzing old ones. My own preference (and here I follow William James) is for narratives in which the parts have a certain amount of "loose play" and which admit contingency and accident as determining factors over narratives consisting of more rigid sequences of events governed by single overarching causal principles. I admit from the start that my preference grows out of social as well as scientific considerations. In a field as esoteric and yet of such everyday concern as paleoanthropology, and one so easily mined for popular theories, what is needed are stories that take account of the full range of possibility in the past and in the future.

This book draws on literary theory, but its results belong to paleoanthropology. Like the more general works in the field, it assumes little background in the study of human evolution. Just as paleoanthropologists engage their audiences by making fossils come alive, I have tried to bring fragments of esoteric texts to life by piecing them together as narratives.

In the opening pages of my Prologue, I engage the reader in a different way—by enacting what the book deals with: the multiple transformations of a single story line. There is a legend common in textbooks, with science as hero going from strength to strength, overcoming dragons of bigotry and superstition, with nature as donor and society as grateful beneficiary. Thomas Henry Huxley worked a variation of this myth, with science as misjudged dragon. This book is cast as a third alternative: science as captive maiden, who if she chooses can take hold of the constraints of narrative and turn them into powerful gifts that may be used for her own benefit and for the benefit of society.

Acknowledgments

For their comments and encouragement given generously at various stages of this book, I would like to thank Mary Ellen Alonso, Linnda Caporael, Richard Levy, and Carolyn Williams.

For their love and enthusiasm, I am grateful to Susan Horton, Icel Massey, my sisters Ricki and Lauren, and, in the home stretch, Tom Schrager.

For their editorial assistance, I thank Ellen Graham and Jehane Kuhn.

I thank my parents, for everything.

Narratives of Human Evolution

Prologue
The Story of
Human Evolution

THE STORY is often told in books on human evolution how, one summer day in 1860, young Thomas Henry Huxley slew Bishop Wilberforce in the Great Debate at Oxford: "A slight tall figure, stern and pale, very quiet and very grave, he stood before us and spoke those tremendous words—words which no one seems sure of now, nor, I think, could remember just after they were spoken, for their meaning took away our breath." No, Huxley said in response to the bishop's mocking question, he would not be ashamed to be descended from a monkey. But he would be "ashamed to be connected with a man who used great gifts to obscure the truth." "No one doubted his meaning, and the effect was tremendous," a witness reported. "One lady fainted and had to be carried out; I, for one, jumped out of my seat" (L. Huxley 1901, 194). And so Huxley's reputation was launched, for as legend has it Huxley's retort "would lend wings to his fame."

Like the myth of Perseus, the winged-shoed rescuer of Andromeda, this early episode in the history of science is often presented as a kind of hero story in which a hero (the scientist) slays a monster (prejudice) and saves a virgin (truth). Huxley himself would use the myth of Perseus and Andromeda to depict the role of science in society, but with the characters redistributed. As he remarked years later in an after-dinner speech to the Royal Academy of Art,

> I think there are many persons who look upon this new birth of our times as a sort of monster rising out of the sea of modern thought with the purpose of devouring the Andromeda of art. And now and then a Perseus with the shoes of swiftness of the ready writer, with the cap of invisibility of the editorial article, and it may be with the Medusa-head of vituperation, shows himself ready to try conclusions with the scientific dragon. Sir, I hope Perseus will think better of it

. . . and here Huxley drew a breath;

> first, for his own sake, because the creature is hard of head, strong of jaw, and for some time past has shown a great capacity for going over and through whatever comes in his way; and secondly, for the sake of justice, for I assure you, of my own personal knowledge that if left alone, the creature is a very debonair and gentle monster. As for the Andromeda of art, he has the tenderest respect for that lady, and desires nothing more than to see her happily settled and annually producing a flock of such charming children as those we see about us. (1883, 682)

Though it urges compassion instead of force, Huxley's version ends, all the same, with science in a dominant position. Indeed, his allegory prefigures a modern myth: that science is a more powerful form of knowledge than art and that any intercourse between the two will be initiated by science.

This book tells a third version. Again, the difference is not in the structure of the tale but in the part played by science. Its purpose is to show that, like Andromeda, paleoanthropology has been held captive by a mighty force. In formulating their theories, paleoanthropologists have been constrained by the rules of art: by mythic archetypes and narrative patterns. With the aid of the reflecting shield of literary theory, scientists may free themselves from these bonds, first, by realizing that they tell stories and, second, by recognizing that they may put them to good purpose. Stories may be strong of jaw, but like Huxley's dragon, they can be serviceable creatures.

The Science of Literature and the Literature of Science

Huxley's version of the myth of science has had a powerful sway, even over students of narrative. The aim of much literary criticism in the past century has been to make the study of literature more scientific. This emphasis on a scientific approach is reflected in the title of one of the classics of twentieth-century literary criticism, Vladimir Propp's *Morphology of the Folktale* (1928). The aim of this book is to classify literary forms, and Russian fairy tales in particular, in the same manner that biologists classify living forms such as plants and animals: "according to their component parts and the relationship of these components to each other and to the whole" (19).

Propp begins his study of the folktale with component parts such as princes, maidens, and dragons, but rather than treat them in isolation, as other scholars had done, he views them in relation to the overall story. Analyzing more than one hundred tales, Propp observes that the same character can perform many different actions. For example, a prince may rescue a maiden in one tale, test her in a second, and threaten her in yet another. Conversely, different characters, however varied they appear, may perform the same action. A prince, a dragon, a farmer, a bear — all may rescue a maiden. "From this we can draw the inference that a tale often attributes identical actions to various personages. This makes possible the study of the tale *according to the functions of its dramatis personae*" (20).

The functions or actions of the dramatis personae are the basic components of the tale. Like the dramatis personae themselves, these actions must be identified in relation to the overall story. As Propp shows, an action can have different meanings depending on where it occurs in the course of a narrative. For example, a hero may slay a dragon to defeat a villain in one tale, to free a maiden in a second, or to pass a test in yet another. On the other hand, Propp points out, certain actions never vary in meaning. A hero may pass a test by slaying a dragon or outwitting a witch, but invariably the hero of the folktale must pass a test. This action—passing a test—is a function of the folktale.

Propp identifies thirty-one consecutive functions of the folktale, each of which can be fulfilled in diverse ways by numerous characters. Each function constitutes a class of items which can fill the same slot in the story. For example,

a dragon ⟶ kidnaps ⟶ a maiden
(or any villain) (or otherwise threatens) (or anything precious)

Seen in this way, an entire narrative can be represented as a string of slots, each open to a variety of alternatives. Conversely, individual stories which seem quite different on the surface might be seen, from this point of view, to possess a similar underlying narrative structure. Propp's study thus has twofold significance: it demonstrates the existence of archetypal narrative patterns, and it provides a method for comparing apparently different narratives.[1]

Just as the European fairy tale has its Andersen and Brothers Grimm, the story of human evolution has its classic authors. Paleoanthropologists are familiar with the names Arthur Keith, Grafton Elliot Smith, Frederic Wood Jones, Henry Fairfield Osborn, and William King Gregory. Though they were the foremost paleoanthropologists of the early twentieth century, all were trained in other fields—the British in medicine (Keith specialized in anatomy, Elliot Smith and his student Wood Jones in neuroanatomy) and the American Osborn and his student Gregory in vertebrate paleontology—and wrote on subjects other than human evolution. Even when writing on fossil man, they addressed a diverse scientific audience: the general readership of *Science* and *Nature*, as well as the more specialized readers of such journals as *Journal of the Royal*

---

1. For discussion of the possible applications, modifications, and limitations of Propp's formalist approach, see Greimas (1970), Lévi-Strauss (1973), Culler (1975), Jameson (1972, 1981), Scholes (1974), Todorov (1981), Bal (1985). Also, Dundes (in Propp 1928 [1968]).

Anthropological Institution, British Medical Journal, Journal of Anatomy, and *Lancet.*

Although the story of human evolution can be traced in even the more specialized journals, it appears most readily in the books of these authors, which appeared following a spate of fossil discoveries in Europe. Though intended for a popular audience, these books—Keith's *The Antiquity of Man* (1915), Elliot Smith's *The Evolution of Man* (1924), Wood Jones's *Arboreal Man* (1916), and Osborn's *Men of the Old Stone Age* (1916)—were not merely popularizations. Often they contained the first complete expression of a scientist's views and were seriously read and reviewed by students of human evolution. This contrasts with the value placed on books in science today. "The scientist who writes one," the philosopher Thomas Kuhn observes, "is more likely to find his professional reputation impaired rather than enhanced" (1970, 20). Even early-twentieth-century paleoanthropologists were sensitive to the risk of writing a book on human evolution. Keith worried that new discoveries would render his books obsolete and that *The Antiquity of Man* would be "put on the shelf," itself an antiquity.

While the Piltdown skull engraved on the cover is enough to keep many paleoanthropologists from seriously consulting the book, the discussion of Piltdown inside *The Antiquity of Man* poses a fresh challenge. Keith's description of the Piltdown skull differs so much from the one found in Elliot Smith's *The Evolution of Man* that one may wonder whether they refer to the same fossil. Like the dragons and princes of Propp's fairy tales, Piltdown can assume very different roles in human evolution, from direct ancestor to distant relative.

This ambiguity extends also to descriptions of events in human evolution. Every paleoanthropological account sets out to answer the question, what really happened in human evolution? Paleoanthropologists generally discuss four main events: a move from the trees to the ground (terrestriality); the development of the upright posture (bipedalism); the development of the brain, intelligence, and language (encephalization); and the development of technology, morals, and society (civilization). Although these events occur in all theories of human evolution, they do not always occur in the same

order (figure 1). Nor do they always have the same significance. If the upright posture develops after the expansion of the brain, this is something different from the upright posture developing before brain expansion. Events have different meanings depending on where they occur in the overall narrative of human evolution, just as the acts of dramatis personae vary according to their places in the folktale.

These differences in ordering are further reflected in the way an event is described. For example, the development of the upright posture is primary in Keith's account: bones, muscles, lungs, spinal nerves, cerebral cortex—even the vasomotor mechanisms controlling blood distribution—are mentioned. Elliot Smith, on the other hand, emphasizes the development of the brain to such an extent that he almost gives the impression that our ancestors had heads but not bodies.

Nevertheless there appears to be some underlying agreement about what happens in human evolution. Just as the hero of a fairy tale fights a battle or slays a dragon to the same end, the human ancestor as seen by Elliot Smith develops a large brain for the same reason that Keith's proto-human becomes bipedal. In formulating their theories of human evolution, these scientists seem to have had in mind a similar narrative pattern which, for present purposes, can be represented by nine functions (figure 2) and read as follows:

Figure 1. Accounts of human evolution usually feature four important episodes: terrestriality, or a shift from the trees to the ground; bipedalism, or the acquisition of the upright posture; encephalization, or the development of the brain, intelligence, and language; civilization, or the emergence of technology, morals, and society. The nature of these events and the order in which they are supposed to have occurred vary from one account to another. According to Darwin, human evolution began when our ancestors, leaving the trees, adopted an upright posture. Other British and American scientists, writing in the early part of this century, held varying views, with Keith and Wood Jones considering bipedalism to be the first important stage, Osborn and Gregory designating terrestriality as first, and Elliot Smith holding that the first stage was encephalization. Gregory's scheme is unusual in placing the use of tools before bipedalism.

6	7	8	9
donor	transformation	test again	triumph

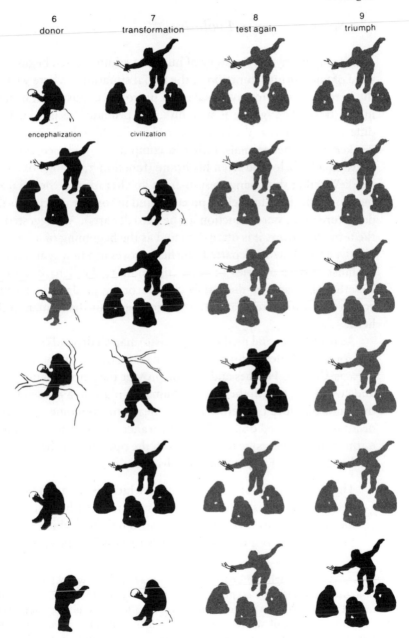

encephalization   civilization

The Story of Human Evolution

Like many myths, the story of human evolution often begins in a state of equilibrium (function 1, the initial situation), where we find the hero leading a relatively safe and untroubled existence, usually in the trees. Though he is a nonhuman primate, he is somehow different (function 2, the hero is introduced). Often he is smaller or weaker than other animals. Either by compulsion or choice, the hero is eventually dislodged from his home (function 3, change of situation). Whether this change results from an alteration in the environment or in the hero himself, it precedes and in some way explains the departure of the hero (function 4, the hero departs). As suggested by the term *departure*, it is often depicted as the beginning of a journey or adventure. Having departed, the hero moves in a new realm where he must survive a series of tests (function 5, the hero is tested). Whether imposed by the harsh climate or by predators or other competitors, these tests are designed to bring out the human in the hero.

As in folktales and myths, this transformation depends on a guiding force or donor, who helps the hero forward. In the myth of Perseus, the gods Hermes and Athena provide the hero with his shield and sword. So, too, in the story of human evolution, a hidden figure or donor provides the hero with the means to overcome his enemy or attain his desired object. The appearance of the donor (function 6, the donor appears) is thus crucial to the outcome of the story. As the literary critic Fredric Jameson observes,

> The donor is therefore the element which explains the change described in the story, that which supplies a sufficiently asymmetrical force to make it interesting to tell, and which is therefore somehow responsible for the "storiness" of the story in the

Figure 2. Although the order of events may vary between paleoanthropological accounts, the events tend to fall into a common narrative structure. This underlying structure can be represented by nine basic actions or "functions," each of which can be filled in several ways. (Events that are latent or continuing from a previous stage are shaded in light gray.)

first place. Thus, the satisfaction and the completeness of the tale comes not from the fact that the hero manages to rescue the princess in the end, but rather from the means or agent given him to do so (a bird who tells him the right word to say to the witch, a magic cloak that lifts him to the tower and so forth). (1972, 67)

The donor may appear in human or animal form, but Jameson shows elsewhere (1981) that it may be the embodiment of a historical force: feudalism, capitalism, class struggle. So, too, evolutionary principles operate as hidden agents in stories of human evolution: natural selection (Darwin, Gregory), orthogenetic factors (Keith, Elliot Smith, Osborn), neo-Lamarckian principles (Wood Jones). These forces bestow on the hero the gifts—intelligence, tools, a moral sense—that transform him into a primitive human (function 7, the hero is transformed).

Still the transformation is not complete, for to prove his humanity the hero must be tested once more (function 8, the hero is tested again). These tests may be imposed by the environment—for example, the rigorous climate of Ice Age Europe—or by the struggle with other humans. In any case, the function of these tests is to raise the hero from a primitive human state to civilization. Given that this was the objective right from the start, the achievement of civilization is the hero's final triumph (function 9, the hero triumphs). Yet there is a final irony, as in many myths. Again and again, we hear how a hero, having accomplished great deeds, succumbs to hubris and is destroyed. In many narratives of human evolution there is a similar sense that man may be doomed: civilization—man's greatest weapon in his struggle with nature—is now his greatest threat. Like many stories, this one draws to a close with the old question of how long man can be successful without succumbing to the forces of destruction within himself.

Scientists may tell stories, even the same story, yet that is not the most important insight to be gained from Propp's method. The main purpose in fitting theories of human evolution into a common framework is not to demonstrate that they fit. On the contrary, it is by examining in what specific ways these theories *differ* from each other that Propp's method is most fruitful. For example, contrasting the narrative functions of bipedalism in the theories of Keith and Elliot Smith can help to clarify the ambiguity which surrounds their discussions of this stage in human evolution. Similarly, comparing the narrative functions filled by fossils, such as Piltdown, provides a way of understanding the different meanings that this fossil held for different authors. Propp's method provides a framework for exploring the conceptual difference between scientific theories.[2]

It provides also a means for revealing their symbolical dimension. A mental sketch will help to prepare the way for this demonstration. The story of human evolution was depicted in figure 2 as a horizontal line of nine functions leading from arboreal to terrestrial, small brain to large brain, savagery to civilization. Just above this horizontal line, there may be pictured a series of gradually rising lines leading from nature to culture, matter to spirit, slavery to freedom. Theories of human evolution, as expressed in the title of a recent book, are about *The Ascent of Man* (Pilbeam 1972). They are hero stories in form and content. They begin with man's lowly origins and end with his triumph over great obstacles. They tell of his struggle with powerful forces in the outside world and in his

---

2.   One of the main assumptions of a narrative approach is that the description of a common underlying structure provides a tool for comparing the manifest differences between narratives (Barthes 1977). Some literary theorists compare the manifest text to the underlying structure itself with the purpose of pointing out contradictions (Jameson 1981; Bal 1985). According to Jameson, Propp's narrative model becomes productive "at the moment when the narrative text in one way or another *deviates* from its basic schema; far less so in those instances where the narrative proving to be its simple replication, the analyst is reduced to noting the conformity of the manifest text to the underlying theoretical schema" (1981, 126). Applying Propp's method to nineteenth-century novels, Jameson shows how, in departing from conventional narrative form, these novels subvert nineteenth-century social and political values. Though the main purpose of this analysis of paleoanthropological texts is to demonstrate how individual texts differ *from each other* rather than from the basic narrative form, it could be argued that, in *not contradicting* the traditional folktale form, scientific texts uphold traditional cultural values. This point is made, in different terms, in the text of this chapter.

own nature. As Alexander Pope sets out in his famous "Essay on Man,"

> Plac'd in this isthmus of a middle state
> A being darkly wise and rudely great
> With too much knowledge for the sceptic side,
> With too much weakness for the stoic pride,
> He hangs between; in doubt to act or rest;
> In doubt to deem himself a god or beast;
> In doubt his Mind or Body to prefer;
> Born but to die, and reas'ning but to err;
>
> . . . .
>
> Created half to rise, and half to fall,
> Great lord of all things, yet a prey to all;

Paleoanthropological texts speak, less poetically perhaps than Pope, of a creature "torn by conflicting desires and propensities," "half-material, half-spiritual—the middle link in the great Chain of Being" (Lovejoy 1936, 103). To follow any single theory of human evolution from beginning to end is to grasp this ancient concept of man as the middle link. That it is presented from a materialistic perspective does not render the image less poignant—indeed the opposite.

Even technical anatomical descriptions reveal hidden meaning when viewed in relation to the overall narrative of human evolution. The freeing of the hands, the shortening of a canine, the rounding of the skull—each may represent the triumph of mind over matter. The narrative of human evolution could in fact be viewed as a sequence of motifs—expanding foreheads and retracting jaws, increasing intellects and diminishing instincts—which forward the plot and are bearers of meaning in themselves (for example, the expanding dominion of mind over matter). Fossil forms may also be arranged as dialectical pairs—Cro-Magnon and Neanderthal, *Australopithecus africanus* and *Australopithecus robustus*. The dominance of Cro-Magnon over Neanderthal, like the struggle between two brothers which occurs in folktale and myth, may represent the triumph of virtue over turpitude.

Little has been said about fossils, those bits of mineralized bone which are usually the main focus of books on human evolution. This exemplifies our working assumption—that theories of human evolution are determined by an apriori set of functions rather than an available set of fossils. Or, in Propp's terms, *what* a tale's dramatis personae do is more basic than *who* does it. According to Propp, a tale's dramatis personae may be defined by what they do—as roles or "spheres of action." Propp identifies several such roles in the folktale (hero, villain, donor). Two spheres of action appear in the story of human evolution: the hero and the donor.[3]

The hero is the protagonist of the tale and yet, defined by his actions, he is a passive creature. He departs, is tested, is transformed, and triumphs, but usually in response to internal or external forces—to the "latent power in his brain" or to "the dwindling of the forests." This is true of many narratives, observes the literary critic Robert Scholes. "The hero is not an agent but a patient. His actions are essentially reactions" (1974, 110). He is more like a thread than a sphere, connecting events "chronologically by moving in time from one to the other, and thematically by the continuous elements in his character" (Scholes and Kellogg 1966, 208). These consecutive phases in the development of the hero could be depicted, like functions, as a linear series: ape-man, pro-dawn man, semi-human, human. (Alternatively, they could be seen as stages—birth, childhood, adulthood—in the life of the hero.) Just as a particular function may be filled by different events (for example, bipedalism or encephalization) the role of the hero at various stages of his adventure can be played by different fossils (Piltdown or Cro-Magnon).

Theories of human evolution differ in their fossil-heroes, but they are alike in having a hero. Similarly, they are alike in having a donor, though not the same one. The role of the donor, the motivating force or prime mover, is played by varying evolutionary agents in early-twentieth-century theories of human evolution.[4] Keith and Elliot

---

3. In stories in which the donor sets the hero a series of tasks, there is no villain: "either a villain or a series of tasks, but not both at once" (Jameson 1972, 65–66).

4. According to Jameson, "what is problematical about Propp's character-functions (hero, donor, villain) . . . emerges when it turns out that we are merely

Smith claimed to be followers of Darwin, and yet they were adherents of orthogenetic principles. They believed—in direct contrast to Darwin's precept that variations arise randomly and are acted on by natural selection—that variations arise and evolve along a fixed or "orthogenetic" course, uninfluenced by environmental conditions.[5] Nor, as the following statements reveal, were they adherents of the same orthogenetic doctrines. According to Keith, "The machinery of evolution works out its untrammelled ends in the embryo" (1923a, 268). According to Elliot Smith, "The steady and uniform development of the brain along a well-defined course . . . must give us the fundamental reason for 'Man's emergence and ascent'" (1924, 20).

"It has been said that I speak of natural selection as an active power or Deity," Darwin wrote in his third edition of *The Origin of Species*; "but who objects to an author speaking of the attraction of gravity as ruling the movements of the planets? Everyone knows what is meant" (Beer 1983, 69). "The problem, of course," as Gillian Beer has observed, "is that every one did *not* know what was meant by natural selection" (69). Even those scientists who identified themselves as Darwinians did not believe natural selection to be the "ruling" force in evolution. Recounting their stories and paying special attention to the imagery of their texts, I hope to show the profound

---

being asked to drop the various elements of the surface narrative into these various prepared slots" (1981, 125). Again, Jameson's object is to show how the surface narrative deviates from the underlying structure. Though the aim is different here, it is also true that the donor can assume a multitude of guises and can even be replaced in a single narrative of human evolution. This is especially evident in the story of Arthur Keith, in which the donor in the guise of nature loses her power over man once he enters the realm of civilization. The ensuing struggle between nature and civilization for control of man can be interpreted as an illustration of the moral of the "middle-link"—"torn by conflicting desires and propensities." This interpretation is in keeping with the idea that theories of human evolution uphold (rather than subvert) traditional values.

5. Though the main purpose here is to demonstrate their departures from Darwinism, it is important to acknowledge that both Keith and Elliot Smith framed their views in direct opposition to the neo-Lamarckians. Their opposition to Lamarck was considerably stronger than that of Darwin, who, as will be shown, accepted that the Lamarckian principles of use-disuse and the inheritance of acquired characteristics may have played a role in human evolution.

theoretical differences which existed between Darwin and his so-called followers. On the other hand, it is precisely by demonstrating that, despite their differences, these theories do follow a common narrative path that I try to show how diverse faiths are served by a single altar.

Part I

Nineteenth-Century Motifs

 OF ALL THE STORIES paleoanthropologists have told, only Darwin's *The Descent of Man* (1871) approaches the status of an authorized version. Like the Bible, it can be read from many points of view.[1] The idea that the human brain came first has been attributed to Darwin as frequently as the idea that the brain came after bipedalism. Perhaps Darwin's book has endured because of its ability to tell many tales. In this section, it tells yet another. The main purpose of this version is not to argue that the brain does or does not come first in Darwin's account but, more important, to demonstrate the fundamental role played by natural selection, especially in contrast to the part it plays in later theories.

The Descent of Man is the preeminent nineteenth-century account, but it was not the first study of human evolution. Works by Huxley, Haeckel, Wallace, Lyell, Vogt, Lubbock, Buchner, and Rolle appeared in the years between Darwin's *The Origin of Species* (1859) and *The Descent of Man*. Huxley's *Man's Place in Nature* (1863)

---

1. The analogy to the Bible holds in another sense. *The Descent of Man and Selection in Relation to Sex* is a "book of books," as the full title indicates. Only the first book is discussed here.

and Haeckel's *The History of Creation* (1868) were the two that had the greatest effect on Darwin. Of the latter Darwin wrote in the preface to *The Descent of Man*, "If this work had appeared before my essay had been written, I should probably never have completed it." Similarly, Darwin acknowledges *Man's Place in Nature* as a ground-breaking work, for "Prof. Huxley . . . has conclusively shewn that in every single visible character man differs less from the higher apes than these do from the lower members of the same order of Primates" (390).

Huxley and Haeckel did help pave the way for Darwin's narrative of human evolution, as will be shown, by supplying a story line and a hero, respectively. But it was Darwin who gave it "storiness" by applying the mechanism of natural selection. Although *The Origin of Species* had made this mechanism available to other writers on human evolution, only Darwin had mastered the principle of natural selection well enough to explain how, exactly, humans evolved from apelike ancestors.

Darwin looms so large in the history of paleoanthropology that he tends to overshadow Huxley and Haeckel. For this reason, I try to present *Man's Place in Nature* in its full novelty, with the mixture of fascination and horror that it might have held for its first readers.

1 *Huxley's Beginning*

"TORN FROM THE HANDS of Mudie's shopmen as if they were novels"[2]—the public response to the 1863 printing of T. H. Huxley's *Man's Place in Nature* reflects the imaginative appeal of early writing on human evolution. Like fantasy, another popular nineteenth-century genre, it depicts an odd world. Its creatures—baboons, gorillas, chimpanzees—are bizarre, but believable. In this world, as in fantasy, there occurs an uncanny event. It turns out that one of these beasts gives birth to an all-too-familiar child. The laws of nature that might allow for such an event had been described only a few years earlier in Darwin's *The Origin of Species* but with little specific reference to humans. Readers of *Man's Place in Nature* might hitherto have believed themselves exempt from Darwinian laws, but they now faced a decision. For them the uncanny event recounted by Huxley must either be an outright fantasy or else it must herald a radical extension of Darwinian principles. In either case, the unthinkable had been thought: humans could be descended from apelike ancestors.

Anticipating his readers' uncertainty as to the nature—fact or fiction?—of the Darwinian view, Huxley begins his book:

2. L. Huxley 1901, 217.

Ancient traditions, when tested by the severe processes of modern investigation, commonly fade away into mere dreams: but it is singular how often the dream turns out to have been a half-waking one, presaging a reality. Ovid foreshadowed the discoveries of the geologist: the Atlantis was an imagination, but Columbus found a western world: and though the quaint forms of Centaurs and Satyrs have an existence only in the realms of art, creatures approaching man more nearly than they in essential structure, and yet as thoroughly brutal as the goat's or horse's half of the mythical compound, are now not only known but notorious. (1863, 9–10)

The manlike apes, foreshadowed by centaurs and satyrs, were themselves an ancient paradox. In folklore and in the works of early scholars, the existence of apes raised the question, could they be degraded men? (Hutchinson 1962, 32). Huxley raises a more frightening possibility: could apes be the ancestors of humans? The insult of ape ancestry was clear to Huxley, who had turned it back on the Bishop of Oxford in their famous debate. In fact, Huxley's famous retort had a greater impact on Huxley himself than on the bishop. While Wilberforce appeared unembarrassed by the incident, it inspired Huxley to pursue the subject of human evolution in a set of "Lectures to Workingmen," which, in turn, became the basis for *Man's Place in Nature.*

Like these lectures, Huxley's book is intended to convince the reader that he is not exempt from nature's law. This conversion would further the spread of Darwinism and, thus, "the mental process of the race": "History shows that the human mind, fed by constant accessions of knowledge, periodically grows too large for its theoretical coverings, and bursts them asunder to appear in new habiliments. . . . Truly the imago state of Man seems to be terribly distant, but every moult is a step gained" (1863, 72). The belief that science will transform humans into higher beings runs through much writing on human evolution, though it is sometimes joined by a pessimistic strand. Huxley would later write, "no study . . . is so utterly saddening as that of the evolution of humanity," but in 1863 none was so grand. With its didactic, almost sermonlike force (the mark of its oral conception) and with its vision of a brave new world order, *Man's Place in Nature* signifies the birth of paleo-anthropology.

The View from Saturn

Huxley's perspective on man is his main contribution to the study of human evolution. Huxley's primary purpose is to establish that humans are part of nature and therefore *did* evolve rather than to show *how* exactly human evolution happened. "In this duty lies my excuse for the publication of these essays. For it will be admitted that some knowledge of man's position in the animate world is an indispensable preliminary to the proper understanding of his relations to the universe" (73). Before the process of human evolution can be described, humans must be seen as animals. This may be achieved in part by humanizing animals—and the first essay of Huxley's book consists of anthropomorphic descriptions of the manlike apes—but it depends largely on transforming the reader's perspective.

Faced with the challenge of changing our minds, Huxley urges us to shed the "mask of humanity" and adopt the viewpoint of an observer from another planet: "let us imagine ourselves scientific Saturnians, if you will, fairly acquainted with such animals as now inhabit the Earth, and employed in discussing the relations they bear to a new and singular 'erect and featherless biped'"(85). To see ourselves as we are, Huxley realizes, we must be something other than human. This irony—that we must be detached in order to see our close connection to nature—is inherent in all forms of self-reflection, from physics to poetry. Huxley combines this "Saturnian irony" with the Socratic irony of a teacher who adopts the limited viewpoint of his pupil. The transition to the truer view is then presented as a journey made by teacher and student.

Like Virgil leading Dante through Hell, Huxley embarks upon his investigation of man's "relations to the underworld of life." Sympathizing with "a certain shock, due, perhaps, not so much to disgust at the aspect of what looks like an insulting caricature, as to the awakening of a sudden and profound mistrust of time-honoured theories," Huxley turns first to the study of development. Comparing the embryos of such animals as the dog, lizard, and frog with those of the ape and the human, Huxley demonstrates their "marvellous correspondence." From this he draws the following lesson: "Without question, the mode of origin and the early stages of the development of man are identical with those of the animals immediately below him in the scale: — without a doubt, in these respects, he is far nearer the Apes, than the Apes are to the Dog" (81). "Startling as the last assertion may appear to be," it appears to Huxley "sufficient to place beyond all doubt the structural unity of man with the rest of the animal world, and more particularly and closely with the apes."

Moving next to the study of comparative anatomy, Huxley once again puts himself at the reader's side and directs his untutored gaze: "look at the flat, narrow haunch bones"; "examine the skull." Beginning with the trunk (vertebral column, ribs, pelvis) and moving to the skull (occipital foramen, supraciliary ridges, cranium, facial bones, jaws, teeth), Huxley agrees that the differences between human and ape appear "vast" and "remarkable" — "at first sight." But with each step (and Huxley moves next to the hand, then the foot and brain), he urges the reader to widen his perspective: to look "lower in the scale," to establish other points of reference. In short, to move closer to Huxley's Saturnian point of view. Until finally, the reader sees "what nature so clearly shows us": that wherever he looks, "the lower Apes and Gorilla would differ more than the Gorilla and the Man."

Again, Huxley's purpose in demonstrating the similarities between humans and apes is to bring the reader to the realization that he is an animal and therefore has evolved. While this "awe-struck voyager may be excused if at first he refuses to believe," by journey's end he has no choice. "Without question, without a doubt," Huxley asserts over and over, humans are part of the natural order. Seeing is believing, and by now the reader has seen for himself. Or has he? Huxley demonstrates the similarities between human and apes, for the most part, without illustrations. Nevertheless, his descriptions create a visual effect. By magnifying the similarities between humans and apes and by minimizing their differences, Huxley draws us closer to his Saturnian perspective.

Huxley saw his argument as a "ranging side by side" of "the facts," and yet one can detect the beginning of a story in his juxtaposition of ape and human. In the shifting back and forth between anatomical structures, Huxley creates a sense of movement from one state to another, each of which is defined in terms of the other (and this is the minimal definition of a narrative). Huxley does not bridge the gap between them with a missing link (like Haeckel); nor does he provide an explanatory middle (like Darwin). But he does lay down a story line. By ascertaining man's true relations to the animate world, he establishes the narrative of human evolution as the passage from ape to human.

Huxley's final goal is to convince us that humans did evolve. Yet his description of this event, which appears toward the end of his essay, is decidedly anticlimactic: "man might have originated, in the one case by the gradual modification of a man-like ape; or in the other case, as a ramification of the same primitive stock" (125). Huxley is ambivalent about the human ancestor and also about the mechanism of human evolution. In a footnote to a discussion of brain size, Huxley speculates about the reason for the difference between humans and apes. "A hair in the balance-wheel, a little rust on a pinion, a bend in a tooth of the escapement, a something so slight that only the practised eye of the watchmaker can discover it" (122). Huxley explains how "some equally inconspicuous structural difference may have been the primary cause of the immeasurable and practically infinite divergence of the Human from the Simian Stirps."

Huxley's watch metaphor—interestingly, a metaphor of defect or malfunction—says little about the mechanics of evolutionary change, but it does reflect, more generally, the doctrine of materialism: the belief that all living phenomena can ultimately be explained according to the physical laws which govern matter. This view is expressed even more vividly in the final passage of his second essay, which for many is the real climax of *Man's Place in Nature*. "In comparing civilized man with the animal world," Huxley observes, "one is as the Alpine traveller, who sees the mountains soaring into the sky and can hardly discern where the deep shadowed crags and roseate peaks end and where the clouds of heaven begin" (131). Just as the geologist teaches that these majestic masses are, "after all, the hardened mud of primeval seas, or the cooled slag of subterranean furnaces—of one substance with the dullest clay, but raised by inward forces to that place of proud and seemingly inaccessible glory . . . the same result will attend the teachings of the naturalist respecting that great Alps and Andes of the living world—Man" (131–32).

Huxley's famous Alpine metaphor, which magically eased the passage of many minds to Darwinism, is in fact a notable sleight-of-hand. It reduces man to matter according to the doctrine of materialism and yet it upholds human dignity by evoking the grandeur and beauty of the tallest mountains. But there is a giveaway: to sustain the reader's dignity Huxley lets in references to a higher and discontinuous realm. It is the "roseate" light and the "clouds of heaven" that transfigure the earthly peaks, whereas the "inward forces" of nature merely raise them to "that place of proud and seemingly inaccessible glory."

In this light, Huxley's imagery reflects aspects of the ancient concept of man as the "middle link" between heaven and earth. This concept is the embodiment of an even more basic philosophical view: the doctrine of dualism which teaches that man has two natures, physical and spiritual. Later Darwin will resolve this paradox by explicitly installing the moral sense in place of man's higher nature—a moral sense which he takes pains to build up from below according to natural principles. For the moment, Huxley spares us the shock of seeing man as entirely earthly. Yet he draws on the familiar image of man as middle link to guide his reader toward precisely this conclusion: that man is "of one substance with the dullest clay" and may be entirely accounted for by physical principles.

Between Mind and Matter

Huxley presents his materialistic beliefs in much the same way that he introduced us to the manlike apes: through ancient images. One might even detect the shadow of the middle link in the half-human centaurs and satyrs of the opening passage. Historically, at least, the beginning to *Man's Place in Nature* could be said to lie with the idea that man is an anomaly, a member of two orders of being—mind and matter. The impetus for Huxley's anatomical comparison of humans and apes, which he undertook before his Oxford debate, was a claim made by Richard Owen that humans belonged to a separate taxonomic subclass, the Archencephala ("of the highest brain"). Owen, the premier British anatomist of the day, was not the first scientist to put humans into a separate taxonomic group. Johann Friedrich Blumenbach and Georges Cuvier, two early nineteenth-century Continental comparative anatomists, had placed humans in a separate order, the Bimana, on the grounds that only humans had two hands and two true feet, whereas apes had four hands and thus belonged in the Quadrumana. Owen tried to deepen this split by arguing that the brains of humans possessed three structures absent in apes: the posterior lobe, the posterior cornu of the lateral ventricle, and the hippocampus minor.

Owen made his claim in 1857. In the same paper he wrote: "I cannot shut my eyes to the significance of that all-pervading similitude of structure—every tooth, every bone, strictly homologous —which makes the determination of the difference between *Homo* and *Pithecus* the anatomist's difficulty" (1857, 20). Owen is ambivalent about the relationship between humans and apes (he emphasizes their similarities and yet in the same paper puts them in separate taxonomic categories), but he clearly saw the homologies between humans and apes as well as Huxley. It was common practice during the early nineteenth century to look for such homologies. By demonstrating the continuities between humans and other species, one demonstrated that life had a "unity of plan," and hence a Planner. The "significance of that all-pervading similitude of structure" to which Owen could not shut his eyes was the existence of an all-pervading Deity.

In the light of this belief Owen undertook a monumental study of the anthropoid apes. Huxley himself refers to Owen's 1835 monograph on the chimpanzees as having "by the carefulness of its comparisons ... made an epoch in the history of our knowledge." But Darwin's *Origin of Species* had created a much greater break. Anatomy became a radically different—indeed, a revolutionary—activity. To demonstrate homologies between humans and apes was now to give evidence of common descent rather than of the existence of a Divine Creator.

With the dramatic change in the "significance of similitude," the determination of the difference between man and ape was more than "the anatomist's difficulty": it became Owen's imperative. If he could demonstrate that these three structures existed only in the human brain, he would establish the truth of Divine Law and specifically the doctrine of special creation, the belief that humans, and all species, were divinely created. Huxley, too, felt morally obliged to compare humans and apes. But his inspiration came from a very different source: the doctrine of materialism. If he could find in the brains of apes the three supposedly missing structures, he would demonstrate that humans were continuous with nature and that their physical and mental makeup could be accounted for entirely by natural principles.

Owen's claim concerning the three anatomical structures lies like a gauntlet at the threshold of *Man's Place in Nature*. Huxley does not take it up, however, until the end of the second essay: "it has been strangely asserted and reasserted" that the human brain alone "exhibits the structures known to anatomists as the posterior lobe, the posterior cornu of the lateral ventricle and the hippocampus minor": "One can only admire the surpassing courage of its enunciator, seeing that it is an innovation which is not only opposed to generally accepted doctrines, but which is directly negatived by the testimony of all original inquirers. . . . It would, in fact, be unworthy of serious refutation, except for the general and natural belief that deliberate and reiterated assertions must have some foundation" (102).

After demonstrating in detail the structural similarities between the brains of humans and apes, in particular the presence of the three structures in question, Huxley concludes: "Any one who cannot see the posterior lobe in an ape's brain is not likely to find a very valuable opinion respecting the posterior cornu or the hippocampus minor. If a man cannot see a church, it is preposterous to take his opinion about its altar-piece or painted window" (118–19). Huxley does not address Owen by name here or, for that matter, anywhere in the second essay. Nevertheless, it is obvious who is being called a blind man (and a liar), just as it was clear who was being made a monkey of in Oxford. The debate between Owen and Huxley was almost as well known to the general public as the debate between Huxley and Wilberforce. Wilberforce was indeed coached by Owen. The sarcasm of this passage was certainly not lost on Huxley's readers: if Owen does not see certain structures of the brain, it is because he studies them through a kind of stained-glass lens—the doctrine of special creation.

Huxley's book begins with a comparison of human and ape, but it gains force from the contest between Huxley and Owen. Described by Huxley as "a battle between Darkness and Light," this debate is inscribed in *Man's Place in Nature*. Huxley wages his struggle in the pages of his book—in its metaphors and myths, in its rhythms and repetitions, in its images and instructions. "The difference between Man and Ape is less than the difference between Ape and Monkey" —over and over the lesson is repeated, like one of the slogans in the *Brave New World* of Huxley's grandson Aldous. Huxley drums it into our heads not only to convince us of the fact but also to counter Owen's "deliberate and reiterated assertion" that they belong to separate taxonomic categories.

Historically, this is the lesson of *Man's Place in Nature*: Huxley's anatomy is based on his differences with Owen as well as on his dissections of apes and humans. The encounter with Wilberforce was another such determining factor: as a result of the Oxford debate, Huxley resolved to study the art of communication. *Man's Place in Nature* gives clear evidence of Huxley's rhetorical skills; it reveals also his belief in the key role played by language in human evolution. As Huxley discloses in the final passage of his second essay, it is through "the marvellous endowment of intelligible and rational speech" that man "has slowly accumulated and organized the experience which is almost wholly lost with the cessation of every individual life in other animals; so that now he stands raised upon it as on a mountain top, far above the level of his humble fellows, and transfigured from his grosser nature by reflecting here and there, a ray from the infinite source of truth" (132). Language is more than art. It is the foundation of all human knowledge. Huxley's belief in the power of science to transform humans into higher beings rests, ultimately, on language. Certainly his ability to transform the reader to his point of view depends on his own linguistic powers. Through irony, Huxley gets us to see what he sees. Through metaphor, he changes our perspective. It is by means of words that appeal to the highest in each of us—the *Saturnian*, the *Alps and Andes*—that we are raised to the truth of human evolution and thereby transformed into higher beings.

Depending on how it is read, *Man's Place in Nature* may belong to more than one genre. With its metaphors and rhythms, it resembles a poem as much as a folktale. The purpose here is to show how Huxley's point-by-point anatomical comparison of human and ape provides a basis for events (such as terrestriality, bipedalism, encephalization, and civilization) and roles (such as Haeckel's ape-man and Darwin's semihuman progenitor) found in later theories of human evolution.

Whether we read it as fantasy or fact, we cannot forget the revolutionary times in which Huxley was writing—"a time of substitution, of new names for old things and new things for old names" (Mackenzie 1973, 54)—and that he wrote the book to attack the doctrine of dualism. Huxley did spread Darwin's word, but he had a deeper message. He was a prophet of the doctrine of materialism and not merely of Darwinian principles.

2   Haeckel's Hero

ERNST HAECKEL was a young man when he became the chief German apostle of evolution. Born a decade after Huxley, he was only thirty-four years old (and already professor of comparative anatomy and zoology at Jena) when he published his famous treatise on evolution, *The History of Creation* (1868). Haeckel's book would mark a turning point in his career, but he believed that Darwin's theory would mark a new epoch in the history of humanity. "Future centuries will celebrate our age, which was occupied with laying the foundations of the Doctrine of Descent, as the new era in which began a period of human development, rich in blessings—a period which was characterized by the victory of free inquiry over the despotism of authority, and by the powerful ennobling influence of the Monistic Philosophy" (1868, 369). Haeckel's defense of Darwin was, like Huxley's, part of a larger campaign against traditional beliefs, in particular the doctrine of dualism. Its overarching purpose was to demonstrate that all phenomena may be explained by a single, or monistic, principle.

Haeckel himself was celebrated by a not-too-distant age: by 1919, the year he died, his books on evolution had sold hundreds of thousands of copies. In 1868, however, he was only at the beginning of his struggle. Haeckel was aware that many readers would reject *The History of Creation* "because more than all others it contradicts the traditional and mythological ideas, and the prejudices which have been held sacred for thousands of years." Haeckel's opening strategy is explicitly modeled after Huxley: "We cannot do better than imagine ourselves with Huxley to be the inhabitants of another planet, who, taking the opportunity of a scientific journey through the universe, have arrived upon earth and have there met with a peculiar two-legged mammal called Man" (265).

Haeckel uses Saturnian irony to prepare us to accept our taxonomic connection with the apes. (He goes one step further than Huxley and puts man not only in the same order as the apes but in the same family.) His final goal is to raise us above our present state: to transform us into naturalists, truly superior to earth's other creatures. Haeckel borrows other vehicles, besides Huxley's interplanetary journey, to accomplish this purpose. In his prediction of a future age "rich in blessings—characterized by the victory of free inquiry over the despotism of authority," Haeckel draws heavily on the old (and inspiring) narrative pattern of struggle, transformation, and triumph found in myths and folktales. Haeckel describes the Doctrine of Descent as "the magic key which would unlock the riddle of the world"; it was by means of rhetorical devices like "magic keys" that Haeckel opened many minds to the truth of evolution.

"How Apes Became Men"

Darwin's theory might cause a revolution in man, but as Haeckel further describes, the evolution of man occurred through slow and steady progress. Haeckel depicts the whole of human history as a long "Chain of Human Progenitors" stretching gradually from the lowest to the highest forms of life. Beginning with the moneron, a creature of "the simplest kind imaginable" (more specifically, "a formless lump of mucous"), Haeckel follows this chain through a series of twenty-one "direct" human ancestors. Having been led through this fantastic span—which ranges from monera through such creatures as amoeba, primeval stomach animals, low worms, skullless animals, single-nostriled animals, mud fish, and gilled- and tailed-amphibians before reaching the mammals—the reader may be ready to agree that "it requires but a slight stretch of the imagination to conceive of an intermediate form" between the highest manlike ape and the lowest human. But this "slight stretch of the imagination" constitutes Haeckel's greatest contribution to paleoanthropology: the first description, from an evolutionary point of view, of a missing link—an extinct species that is transitional between apes and humans.

Pithecanthropus alalus, the speechless ape-man, was not entirely a figment of Haeckel's imagination. Like most nineteenth-century intermediate forms it was constructed according to principles derived from the studies of paleontology, comparative anatomy, and embryology. Still, no fossil remains fitting Haeckel's description had yet been discovered.

> We know of no fossil remains of the hypothetical primaeval man . . . who developed out of anthropoid apes during the tertiary period, either in Lemuria or in southern Asia, or possibly in Africa. But considering the extraordinary resemblance between the lowest woolly-haired men, and the highest man-like apes, which still exist at the present day, it requires but a slight stretch of the imagination to conceive an intermediate form connecting the two, and to see in it an approximate likeness to the supposed primaeval men, or ape-like men. The form of their skull was probably very long, with slanting teeth; their hair wooly; the colour of their skin dark, of a brownish tint. The hair covering the whole body was probably thicker than in any of the still living human species; their arms comparatively longer and stronger; their legs, on the other hand, knock-kneed, shorter and thinner, with entirely undeveloped calves. (326-27)

Compared to Haeckel's later detailed portraits which depict ape-men as racially variable (reflecting his polygenic belief that human races have evolved separately from diverse apelike ancestors), Haeckel's description appears a preliminary sketch. Nevertheless, it establishes the most distinctive characteristic of such ape-men. "These ape-like men . . . originated out of the Man-like Apes, or Anthropoides, by becoming completely habituated to an upright walk" (293). Ape-men might be straight-haired or woolly, dark-skinned or fair, but from their first appearance in 1868 they would walk, more or less, bipedally.

Like everything else in Haeckel's book, the transformation to the upright posture occurs "slowly, gradually and step by step." "By the fore feet more and more exclusively adopting and retaining the function of grasping and handling, and the hinder feet more and more exclusively the function of standing and walking, there was developed that contrast between the hand and foot which is indeed not exclusively characteristic of man, but which is much more strongly developed in him than in the apes most like men" (299–300). Haeckel reminds us that apes have two hands instead of four primarily to contradict Blumenbach and Cuvier, who placed the apes in the Quadrumana. Yet elsewhere he writes: "The forehand of the Anthropoides became the human hand, their hinder hand became a foot." Haeckel further develops this contrast between the hand and foot:

> This differentiation of the fore and hinder extremities was . . . not merely most advantageous for their own development and perfecting, but it was followed at the same time by a whole series of very important changes in other parts of the body. The whole vertebral column, and more especially the girdle of the pelvis and shoulders, as also the muscles belonging to them, thereby experienced those changes which distinguish the human body from that of the most man-like apes. (300)

The differentiation of the hand and foot is clearly the impetus for the development of the upright posture. Yet Haeckel's description moves in a circular fashion from this point. Though anatomical changes "follow at the same time," like spokes in a wheel, these changes seem to be directed inwardly toward "their own development and perfecting," as in the initial differentiation of the hand and foot, rather than toward any Darwinian advantage, such as greater success in finding food or avoiding predators.

Given Haeckel's description, it is possible to imagine ape-men in various stages of erectness, but it is difficult to discern why the ape-man stands up in the first place. Haeckel describes *what* happens, by what anatomical changes the erect posture evolves, but he does not say *how* bipedalism evolves, by what mechanism, or *why*, in response to what new need or opportunity. If we knew what was being grasped by the forehands, we might know why it was "advantageous." But Haeckel does not say what they hold or where the hinder feet stand or tread. Elsewhere Haeckel observes that humans can use their feet to climb trees and even to weave and row, but this is to demonstrate the similarities between apes and humans (and thus to corroborate Huxley's thesis concerning their close taxonomic relationship) rather than to explain their differences. In *The Descent of Man*, Darwin acknowledges Haeckel's "excellent discussion of the steps by which man became a biped," yet Haeckel makes little reference to Darwin's principle of natural selection in his discussion. Haeckel's discussion invokes Lamarck's principle of use-disuse as much, if not more, than Darwin's mechanism of natural selection.

Origins of Language and the Mind

Following the upright posture, the most important stage in human evolution is the origin of articulate language which "must, more than anything else, have had an ennobling and transforming influence upon the mental life of Man, and consequently upon his brain." It is language, Haeckel continues, and "the higher differentiating and perfecting of the larynx" that "helped to create the deep chasm between man and animal." Language is connected with "the differentiating and perfecting of the larynx" in the same manner that the development of the upright walk is correlated with the differentiation of the fore- and hindlimbs. "The important perfecting of these organs and their functions must have necessarily and powerfully reacted upon the differentiation of the brain and the mental activities dependent upon it, and thus have paved the way for the endless career in which Man has since progressively developed, and in which he has far outstripped his animal ancestors" (299).

Man's superiority rests on a solid material base: the limbs and the larynx. Nevertheless, the development of these structures appears tentative in Haeckel's description. Though Haeckel refers to their combined effects, he does not draw a connection between them except to say that the development of language followed long after the upright posture. Nor is it clear how, exactly, the differentiation of the larynx affects the development of the brain. As Haeckel describes, the larynx "necessarily and powerfully reacted upon the differentiation of the brain and the mental activities dependent upon it," but elsewhere the mind appears to be the cause of articulate language: "a real language of words or ideas, a so-called 'articulate' language," is one in which "abstraction changes sounds into words, and words into sentences." But whence abstraction?

Haeckel is sketchy about the origins of mind; perhaps he was trying to avoid "the erroneous and dualistic philosophies of past times," rather than to skirt a difficult issue. His description of the brain as passive—acted upon by the "differentiation and perfecting" of the larynx and the limbs—is in sharp and significant contrast to the doctrine of special creation, which views reason as the primary agent or "divine spark" in human origins. Later, Haeckel does "cast a glance at the mental development of Man to show that it too is subject to the great general law of development." Using studies of the mental life of children and "wild savages," Haeckel demonstrates that the human mind or soul "develops from the beginning, step by step and gradually, just like the body."

> In a newly born child we see that it possesses neither an independent consciousness, nor in fact clear ideas. These arise only gradually when, by means of sensuous experience, the phenomena of the outer world affect the central nervous system. But still the little child is wanting in all those differentiated emotions of the soul which the full-grown man acquires only by the long experience of years. From this graduated development of the human soul in every single individual we can, in accordance with the inner causal connection between ontogeny and phylogeny, directly infer the gradual development of the human soul in

all mankind, and further, in the whole of the vertebrate tribe. (361)

Once again, the great law of development governing the mind appears to work in a way that is closer to Lamarck's principle of use-disuse than to Darwin's natural selection. As described, it also exemplifies Haeckel's own famous principle of recapitulation, which describes "the inner causal connection between ontogeny and phylogeny"—that is, between the development of the individual and the evolution of the species as a whole. Haeckel also uses this principle to account for the mental differences between "lower" and "higher species" of men. As Haeckel explains, the "wild savages," with their rudimentary language, poorly developed powers of abstraction, and uncivilized practices, "have barely risen above the lowest stage of transition from man-like apes to ape-like men, a stage which the progenitors of the higher human species had already passed through thousands of years ago" (364).

Though Haeckel's account is structured by "the inner causal connection between ontogeny and phylogeny," it lacks the specific causal connections between character, action, and setting that one expects in narrative. Even so, one can see the beginnings of a story in his chain of ancestors (ape, ape-man, human races) and in his series of loosely connected events (upright posture, language, encephalization). Given Haeckel's belief in polygenism (a belief that many saw as divisive and discriminatory but which Haeckel saw as unifying), human evolution could be depicted as this same story reenacted, each time beginning with a different ape-man and ending with a different race of present day humans.

As for the setting, it is unclear where, exactly, the story begins. Haeckel does not link the development of the upright posture to terrestriality, although he does attribute the lack of *Pithecanthropus* fossil remains to arboreal habits. Haeckel predicts that these remains will be found in Asia, but this is because of the geographical distribution of living apes and human races (and also of human languages), not because environmental factors, such as the hot, humid climate of southern Asia or the dense flora and fauna, are invoked to play a role in the ape-man's struggle to survive. Elsewhere, Haeckel attributes the degeneration of some human races to "unfavorable conditions of existence" (332) and to competition from other races, but for the most part, Haeckel's human progenitors appear to live relatively unthreatened lives.

Indeed, man's place in Haeckel's account appears more like a protected corner inside a scientist's lab than a precarious niche in the wild world of Darwin. The most dangerous natural feature in Haeckel's book is the "deep chasm between man and animal" in the mind of his nineteenth-century reader. Haeckel's missing link is designed to bridge this gap, and yet *Pithecanthropus alalus*—passive and unused to strife—seems hardly adequate for the kind of struggle for existence that animals encounter in Darwin's *The Origin of Species*. Although Darwin would test this unpromising creature in *The Descent of Man* and, by means of natural selection, equip him with the resources needed to triumph over all obstacles, Haeckel's ape-man is not yet a hero. If there is a hero in Haeckel's book, it is the reader who, by overcoming traditional ideas and joining the struggle against dualism, may become a higher form of human.

3 Darwin's Donor

THOUGH HUXLEY and Haeckel prepared the way for *The Descent of Man*, Darwin was his own prophet. In the conclusion to *The Origin of Species*, Darwin predicts the consequences of his general theory of evolution: "In the future I see open fields for far more important researches. Psychology will be securely based on the foundation already well laid by Mr. Herbert Spencer, that of the necessary acquirement of each mental power and capacity by gradation. Much light will be thrown on the origin of man and his history" (1859/1948, 374). Darwin published his monumental work on man only twelve years later, but in fact, he had been working on the problem of human evolution for decades. He began his notebook on "Man, Mind, and Materialism" in the summer of 1838, when Haeckel was four years old and Huxley was fourteen. Darwin's views on man were crucial to the formulation of his general theory, but his omission of them in the *Origin* was critical to its acceptance. So sensitive was the issue of human evolution that Darwin considered excluding any reference to humans. Though he does include it, Darwin's famous remark—that "light would be thrown"—hides more than it reveals: by 1859 the fact of human evolution was, for Darwin, a premise rather than a prediction.

Darwin does not present his own doctrine of descent as the next step on Spencer's ladder of mental growth, but like Huxley and Haeckel, he does appeal to the reader's higher intellect in making his argument. Throughout *The Descent of Man*, Darwin addresses himself to the naturalist who would view himself "in the same spirit as he would any other animal," and whose "unbiased mind" cannot study "any living creature, however humble, without being struck with enthusiasm at its marvellous structure and properties." He appeals also to our desire for moral improvement, for the "disinterested love for all living creatures" is the noblest human attribute. Like Huxley, Darwin correlates moral and intellectual superiority with a comprehensive view, but where Huxley used distance, Darwin uses intimacy—identification with the lowly and unobserved —to persuade the reader. The naturalist is the reader-hero of Darwin's book, but even he will need to make a special effort to overcome the "natural pride and arrogance which made our forefathers declare that they were descended from demigods." Still Darwin is optimistic that rationality will prevail and that "the time will before long come, when it will be thought wonderful that naturalists, who were well acquainted with the comparative structure and development of man, and other mammals, should have believed that each was the work of a separate act of creation" (1871/1948, 495).

Darwin's prediction of a future world joined in the love of nature and truth sounds a calm Arcadian note after the ebullient prophesies of Huxley and Haeckel. But Darwin's depiction of the human past, especially in contrast to Haeckel's lablike world, is anything but tranquil: with its "cold dry climates" and "hot tropical forests" full of "dangerous beasts," and "physical hardship"; with its mountains, volcanoes, islands, and open plains, which human progenitors cross in "incessant migrations," engaging in "ceaseless struggle"—it is the scene of movement, strife, and activity. But it is a place of controlled activity in which human actions obey natural laws and, in particular, the "rigid law of natural selection." Like the hand of Providence in the biblical account, natural selection justifies even where it fails to explain. What happens is not always "right" or well understood, but it is "fit" and, ultimately, intelligible. Darwin's world is not often a nice place, but it is a rational one.

"In the earlier editions of my *Origin of Species* I perhaps attributed too much to the action of natural selection," Darwin confesses in chapter 2 of *The Descent of Man* (441). Throughout his discussion of human evolution, Darwin makes a point of introducing other causal principles (such as direct action of the environment, correlated variation, economy of growth, arrests of development, the acquired effects of use and disuse), though the principle of natural selection, or "struggle for existence," remains the chief agent of evolution. Like these other causal principles, natural selection explains events according to their antecedent or "efficient causes" (predators, competition, climate). But it also explains events according to their consequences or "final causes" (fitness, survival, adaptive success). In this latter aspect, natural selection may appear to operate in a teleological fashion, as though directed toward some overall design or purpose.[1] Though Darwin uses natural selection mostly as an efficient cause, he confesses that he does believe human evolution has been toward a preferred and higher state; "that progress has been much more general than retrogression; that man has risen, though by slow and interrupted steps from a lowly condition to the highest standard as yet attained by him in knowledge, morals and religion" (511).

Huxley and Haeckel had similarly described human evolution as an uplifting account: the gradual rise of humans from lowly origins. But they structured their accounts taxonomically, according to the *scala naturae*, or the great chain of being that orders all living things, whereas Darwin deploys a chain of events rather than a chain of beings. His chain is, in fact, a flexible series of joined elements, each of which has multiple causes and consequences. Each element Darwin describes, even those he acknowledges as not fully understood, is ultimately correlated with every other, if not by natural selection then by other principles. Nor is the story complete without all of

---

1. The teleological aspects of the principle of natural selection have been widely discussed and in most cases are based on a misinterpretation of Darwin. See Ayala and Dobzhansky (1974), Gould (1977), Hull (1974), Sober (1984), Williams (1966).

them. It is this causal relationship between elements that distinguishes Darwin's account from its predecessors. Whereas Huxley presents a juxtaposition of anatomical points and Haeckel describes a series of loosely connected structural changes (differentiation of limbs, differentiation of larynx), Darwin presents a network of themes (bipedalism, encephalization, civilization), each of which consists of interrelated motifs held together by efficient and final causes.

Like most narratives, the story of human evolution is subject to an intrinsic "teleological determinism" (Culler 1975, 209): elements are presented not as they occur but as they contribute to the outcome of the story. The end is present throughout the work. Darwin's account is both more purposive and more ambiguous than its predecessors. It is the recurrence of individual elements and their polyvalence—their ability to combine in multiple ways—that, as Gillian Beer observes, gives Darwin's conception such "extraordinary hermeneutic potential—the power to yield a great number of significant meanings."[2]

Many stories are told in *The Descent of Man*, and yet it is difficult to read "for the story." Darwin's conception of human evolution does not appear as a single sequence but, like the rudimentary anatomical structures presented in the first chapter, in partial traces and fragments. It is no less of a narrative for that reason. Even in novels, the story rarely comes whole or in sequence. Poems may have a beginning, middle, and end but, as Truffaut said of his films, not necessarily in that order. Darwin makes his first reference to the birthplace of man while discussing the rudiments of the ear, but it is not until chapter 6 that he discusses it fully. On the other hand, the table of contents reveals the outlines of a story.

Chapter I The evidence of the descent of man from some lower form (terrestriality)

Chapter II On the manner of development from some lower form (bipedalism)

2. "The multiplicity of stories implicit in evolution was *in itself* an element in its power over the cultural imagination: what mattered was not only the specific stories it told, but the fact that it told many and diverse ones" (Beer 1983, 114).

Chapter III and Chapter IV Comparison of the mental powers of man and the lower animals (encephalization)

Chapter V On the development of the intellectual and moral faculties (civilization)

The order of presentation does not necessarily reflect an evolutionary sequence, but it does follow Darwin's suggestion that progress has been from the perfection of the human body to "the highest standard as yet attained by him in knowledge, morals and religion" (511).

ARBOREALITY: in which (1) *the scene is set* in some "warm, forest-clad land," and (2) *the hero is introduced*, "weak and defenceless."

And so we find in chapter 1 a beginning to the story. Like many mythical beginnings, it presents a scene of security, plenitude, and no rivalry. On the basis of rudiments, in particular a rudimentary lobule on the human ear (later called "Darwin's point"), Darwin supposes that our ancient ancestors "were but little exposed to danger and so during a lengthened period moved their ears but little, and thus gradually lost the power of moving them." Darwin is not entirely satisfied with this explanation (perhaps because of its Lamarckian flavor), and yet a similar argument is drawn from man's limited sense of smell, which in other animals is a means of detecting danger. This impression is reinforced in later chapters. "Judging from the condition of the great toe in the (human) foetus," Darwin observes in chapter 6, "our progenitors, no doubt, were arboreal in their habits, and frequented some warm, forest-clad land" (524). When discussing the "small strength and speed of man, his want of natural weapons" at the end of chapter 2, he notes that man's ancestors "would not have been exposed to special danger even if far more helpless and defenceless than any existing savages, had they inhabited some warm continent or large island" (527).

The notion "that man is one of the most helpless and defenseless creatures in the world; and that during his early and less well developed condition he would have been still more helpless" was very popular at the time *The Descent of Man* was written. As Darwin himself pointed out, it had been used to attack his theory.

> The Duke of Argyll, for instance, insists that "the human frame has diverged from the structure of the brutes, in the direction of greater physical helplessness and weakness. That is to say, it is a divergence which of all others it is most impossible to ascribe to mere natural selection." He adduces the naked and unprotected state of the body, the absence of great teeth and claws for defense, the small strength and speed of man and his slight power of discovering food or avoiding danger by smell. (443)

Like Richard Owen, the Duke of Argyll was a major opponent of human evolution, but he appears in *The Descent of Man* less as an antagonist than a foil. Darwin introduces Argyll's claim to turn it to his own advantage. For though "we do not know whether man is descended from some small species, like the chimpanzee, or from one as powerful as the gorilla . . . We should, however, bear in mind that an animal possessing great size, strength, and ferocity, and which, like the gorilla, could defend itself from all enemies, would not perhaps have become social: and this would most effectually have checked the acquirement of the higher mental qualities, such as sympathy and the love of his fellows. Hence it might have been an immense advantage to man to have sprung from some comparatively weak creature" (444).

Darwin was not the first to suggest that the weak might inherit the earth, but he was the first to show how they might do so by natural selection. This idea of development from humble or handicapped origins (a common feature of folktale and myth) can also be found in later paleoanthropological accounts and is often associated with a Rousseauistic "state of nature" or youthful innocence. It is also associated with the idea of the misfit or runt who, lacking all the usual natural resources (size, strength, teeth and claws), chooses or is compelled to play by unconventional rules. Though Darwin usually manages to keep them under the control of natural selection, his human progenitors live a kind of bohemian existence. As we will see, they make love and war by inventing their own laws of behavior.

TERRESTRIALITY: in which (3) *the hero's situation changes* due to a "change in its manner of procuring subsistence, or some change in the surrounding conditions."

Whether by compulsion or choice, Darwin's early human progenitor is eventually dislodged from its arboreal home. As a result of "a change in its manner of procuring subsistence, or some change in the surrounding conditions" (433), it becomes "less arboreal" and lives "more and more" on the ground. Darwin does not specify the immediate cause of this event, nor does he describe the steps by which it happens (though it is probably gradual—"more and more," "less and less"), but he suggests that it is probably related to diet. Success, in the long run, is measured by numbers of offspring, and "numbers depend primarily on the means of subsistence." Darwin does not say what, exactly, man's remote ancestor ate, but "he probably inhabited a hot country; and this would have been favorable for a frugiferous diet, on which, judging from analogy, he subsisted." His feeding habits probably became more diversified with the shift to the ground, for man in even the "rudest state" has a varied diet. "He has invented and is able to use various weapons, tools, traps, etc., with which he defends himself, kills or catches prey, and otherwise obtains food. He has made rafts or canoes for fishing or crossing over to neighboring fertile islands. He has discovered the art of making fire, by which hard and stringy roots can be rendered digestible, and poisonous roots or herbs innocuous" (496). Darwin describes here a later stage of human evolution, but even at a remoter stage, it is likely that a change in the means of subsistence preceded the change in diet. As we will see, from the moment their feet touch the ground, the evolutionary success of these ancestral creatures depends on the degree to which they make tools and other instruments.

Like many mythical departures, the shift to the ground signifies the beginning of a journey. It is a passage from one situation (of safety and prosperity) to another almost antithetical one (scarcity and danger). This occurs in many narratives: the initial setting serves as a contrasting background for the ensuing adventure (Frye 1976, 53). This change in setting, in turn, serves as a catalyst for the transformation of the hero, with the result that, compared with his arboreal ancestors, he too is an antithesis.

	ARBOREAL	TERRESTRIAL
HABITAT	abundant food	scarce food
	little predation	much predation
	refuge	danger
	complacency	challenge
HABIT	frugivorous	omnivorous
	peaceable	aggressive
	lazy	vigilant
	arrested	progressive

While the shift from the trees to the ground is the immediate or efficient cause of the passage from ape to human, it results also in the transformation of the terrestrial world itself: from a state of nature to a state of art. It is through artifice that man's ancestors survive the shift and, eventually, through the practice of architecture and agriculture that man recreates the security and prosperity of his ancestral paradise. Even before these Promethean acts there is a sense of human defiance of the order of the natural world. Though they are ground dwelling, man's ancestors never really live like other terrestrial animals. Thrown into a world for which they are ill equipped, they find strength in numbers rather than in individual prowess. The move to the ground thus coincides almost immediately with a shift to the group, but it leads also to a deeper split. Whereas individuals in nature are subject to the law of struggle for existence, individuals within groups behave according to a second antithetical law: the principle of mutual aid and defense.

Life for the semihuman progenitor, then, is divided into two terrestrial realms: *inside* and *outside* the group. Life inside the group in many ways resembles the lost arboreal realm: nurturing, loving, warm. Outside the group, life is characteristically terrestrial: dangerous and harsh. Even here, man's ancestors are set apart from other terrestrial animals. Their greatest threat is not the claws and teeth of lone predators but the clubs and spears of other tribes. According to Darwin, "natural selection arising from the competition of tribe with tribe . . . would, under favourable conditions, have sufficed to raise man to his present high position in the organic scale" (444). It is by his own hand, we shall see, that man benefits and suffers.

BIPEDALISM: in which (4) *the hero departs* from the apes by becoming "more and more erect."

The development of the upright posture is introduced in chapter 2. As Darwin describes, it follows almost immediately after the shift to the ground. "As soon as some ancient member in the great series of Primates came to be less arboreal, owing to a change in its manner of procuring subsistence, or to some change in the surrounding conditions, its habitual manner of progression would have been rendered more strictly quadrupedal or bipedal" (433–34). The move to the ground is an immediate but not a sufficient cause of bipedalism, for as Darwin suggests, it could also have resulted in quadrupedalism. A more decisive starting point appears in chapter 4 with the differentiation of the fore- and hindlimbs.

Man could not have attained his present dominant position in the world without the use of his hands which are so admirably adapted to act in obedience to his will. Sir C. Bell insists that "the hand supplies all instruments, and by its correspondence with the intellect gives him universal dominion." But the hands and arms could hardly have become perfect enough to manufacture weapons, or to have hurled stones and spears with a true aim as long as they were habitually used for locomotion and for supporting the whole weight of the body, or . . . so long as they were especially fitted for climbing trees. Such rough treatment would also have blunted the sense of touch, on which their

> delicate use largely depends. From these causes alone it would
> have been an advantage to man to become a biped; but for many
> actions it is indispensable that the arms and whole upper part of
> the body should be free; and he must for this end stand firmly on
> his feet. (434)

Both Darwin and Haeckel begin their discussions of bipedalism with
the differentiation of the hands and feet, but from this point their
discussions diverge significantly. Whereas Haeckel, wary of any
dualistic hint, was reluctant to draw a connection between the evolution of bipedalism and intelligence, Darwin makes such a connection central. Indeed, Darwin links mind and body much as Michel-
angelo joins man and God on the ceiling of the Sistine Chapel: by
the hand. As Darwin tells the story, it is by the use of his hands,
acting in service to his will, that man reaches his upright—and
dominant—position.

Bipedalism appears to be a way of advancing the mind more
than a means of moving the body. "As the hands became perfected
for prehension, the feet should have become perfected for support
and locomotion," Darwin observes, yet the arms appear to move
more than the hindlimbs in the above passage. Man's ancestors became bipeds to hurl stones and spears (and thus to hold their ground),
rather than to chase prey or flee from the teeth and claws of predators. At one point Darwin does discuss gait, but this is to defend his
account of gradual change, not to present the uses of bipedal
locomotion.

> If the gorilla and a few allied forms had become extinct, it might
> have been argued an animal could not have been gradually con-
> verted from a quadruped to a biped, as all the individuals in an
> intermediate condition would have been miserably ill-fitted for
> progression. But we know (and this is well worthy of reflection)
> that the anthropomorphous apes are now actually in an inter-
> mediate condition; and no one doubts that they are on the whole
> well adapted for their conditions of life. Thus the gorilla runs
> with a sidelong shambling gait, but more commonly progresses
> by resting on its bent hands. The long armed apes occasionally

use their arms like crutches, swinging their bodies forward between them, and some kinds of Hylobates, without having been
taught, can walk or run upright with tolerable quickness; yet
they move awkwardly. (434–35)

Darwin uses the living apes to show how bipedalism might have
gradually evolved, and yet—awkward and shambling, using their
arms like crutches—they look more like halting invalids than incip-
ient bipeds.

Darwin's discussion of the steps by which man became bipedal
departs from Haeckel's and, at the same time, seems to turn aside
from the Darwinian line of reasoning. The division of labor between the limbs appears to be drawn along dualistic lines. This impression is due, perhaps, to the way Darwin describes the origin of
bipedalism as a kind of flashback, taking man's "present dominant
position" as a premise. Yet like Huxley, Darwin acknowledges man's
dominance only to reduce it to a material basis. Though man's hands
"act in obedience to the will," they did not evolve for that reason; as
Darwin showed, their delicate use depended in the first place on the
sense of touch. The human hand originated in response to the need
to touch trees rather than to the touch of the Creator, as in Michel-
angelo's rendering.

Nevertheless, the development of the upright posture is a special
—indeed a unique—event: as Darwin remarks, "Man alone is a
biped." Bipedalism is the means by which man breaks away from the
rest of the animal world, if not from the laws of nature.

ENCEPHALIZATION: in which (5) *the hero is tested* in a battle
of wits; (6) *aided by his donor*, natural selection, he is (7) *transformed*
into an intelligent and almost human creature.

Once launched on his own two feet, man marches toward his
destiny, for the most part, by the force of his intellect. As Darwin
observes at the end of chapter 2,

The ancestors of man were, no doubt, inferior in intellect and
probably in social disposition to the lowest existing savages; but

it is quite likely that they might have existed, or even flourished, if they had advanced in intellect while gradually losing their brute-like powers, such as that of climbing trees, etc. But these ancestors would not have been exposed to any special danger, even if far more helpless and defenceless than any existing savages, had they inhabited some warm continent or large island, such as Australia, New Guinea, or Borneo, which is now the home of the orang. And natural selection arising from the competition of tribe with tribe, in some such large area as one of these, together with the inherited effects of habit, would, under favourable conditions, have sufficed to raise man to his present high position in the organic scale. (444)

As Darwin describes, man takes his first steps on the ground un-threatened by natural predators. Nor is he bothered much by them later. The real struggle in *The Descent of Man* occurs not between animals and men but between humans of varying intellects.

Darwin's approach to the evolution of intelligence will depend on emphasizing the mental differences between men; he begins by minimizing the mental differences between humans and other animals. "My object," Darwin announces at the beginning of chapter 3, "is solely to shew that there is no fundamental difference between man and the higher mammals in their mental faculties." Building on the foundation laid by Herbert Spencer, Darwin devotes much of this chapter and the next to showing how the higher mental powers (reason, language, sense of beauty, belief in God) develop from the lower (imitation, memory, attention) by gradation. Though Darwin disagrees with Cuvier's belief that instinct and intelligence stand in inverse ratio, he does link intelligence to a decrease in fixed or in-stinctive patterns of behavior. "Little is known about the functions of the brain, but we can perceive that as the intellectual powers become highly developed, the various parts of the brain must be connected by very intricate channels of the freest communication; and as a consequence each separate part would perhaps tend to be less well fitted to answer to particular sensations or associations in a definite and inherited—that is instinctive—manner" (447). Like the hand, the human brain has become "freed" to perform a wider range of functions. Indeed, the hand expands the power of the brain even further. As shown earlier, the freeing of the hands allows man to manufacture weapons and tools and thus to develop one of his greatest mental abilities: the power of invention.

Though man's ingenuity seems to have instinctive force—and Darwin attributes the diversity of man's languages to his "love of novelty"—it is largely a function of his intellect. As Darwin describes, the inventions "by which man in the rudest state has become so pre-eminent, are the direct results of his powers of observation, memory, curiosity, imagination and reason" (494). These faculties are found in other animals but are fostered, in man, as a result of his propensity for living among his fellows: "as soon as the progenitors of man became social (and this probably occurred at a very early period), the principle of imitation, and reason and experience would have increased and much modified the intellectual powers in a way of which we see only traces in the lower animals" (497).

Man's intellectual powers are not so much transformed by social life as amplified. Imitation does not require much reasoning power, and as Darwin describes, inventions may spread by habitual or mindless practice.

> Now if some one man in a tribe, more sagacious than the others, invented a new snare or a weapon, or other means of attack or defence, the plainest self-interest, without the assistance of much reasoning power, would prompt the other members to imitate him; and thus all would profit. The habitual practice of each new art must likewise in some slight degree strengthen the intellect. If the new invention were an important one, the tribe would increase in number, spread and supplant other tribes. In a tribe thus rendered more numerous there would always be a rather greater chance of the birth of other superior and inventive members. If such men left children to inherit their mental superiority, the chance of the birth of still more ingenious members would be somewhat better, and in a very small tribe decidedly better. (497–98)

The intellect may be strengthened "in some slight degree" by each member of a tribe imitating and practicing new arts, as Darwin describes, but new arts depend, ultimately, on the birth of "superior and inventive members." Inventions may spread by the principle of imitation but *inventiveness* is the result of natural selection operating on the mental variations between individuals.

Man's intellect supplies him with the means to extend his dominion in the world, but it obeys a greater power. In raising the level of competition of tribe with tribe, it acts in service to natural selection. It is here that the role of natural selection as donor is especially apparent. Man could not have attained dominance in the world without the use of his hands and brain, but he acquires his hands and brain by the operation of natural selection.

Though man's first inventions probably originate by chance events (for according to Darwin there is much truth in John Lubbock's suggestion "that tool-making may first have been accidental"), they may also arise in the same way that they spread, by the principle of imitation: Darwin suggests that the first inventions may represent attempts to imitate the natural instruments of stronger animals. With competition among tribes, however, men set their own standards. As the struggle for existence is escalated into the art of war, their weapons become more dangerous than the teeth and claws of even the fiercest predators. So fully does his mind compensate for his physical shortcomings that, eventually, man's teeth undergo a reduction.

"Of the high importance of the intellectual faculties there can be no doubt," Darwin concludes. "We can see, that in the rudest state of society, the individuals who were the most sagacious, who invented and used the best weapons or traps, and who were best able to defend themselves, would rear the greatest number of offspring." Of all man's inventions, however, the greatest is language. It is on language that man's "wonderful advancement" toward civilization has mainly depended. Though language may be traced to strong emotional and instinctive roots (Darwin refers to the "half-art, half-instinct" of language), it is largely a function of his higher mental powers. As Darwin observes, "The mental powers in some early progenitor of man must have been more highly developed than in any existing ape, before even the most imperfect form of speech could have come into use." Other parts of the body must also have undergone a change for, like Haeckel, Darwin ascribes a large role to the differentiation and continued use of the vocal organs. Like man's hands, the vocal organs may have been guided, at first, by the principle of imitation. As Darwin suggests, "may not some unusually wise ape-like animal have imitated the growl of a beast of prey, and thus told his fellow-monkeys the nature of the expected danger?" (463). Elsewhere Darwin speculates that language originated, like other inventions, in response to competition from other humans rather than to predation from other animals. "When we treat of sexual selection we shall see that primeval man, or rather some early progenitor of man probably first used his voice in producing true musical cadences, that is in singing" (463).

Man's mental powers might be acquired not just by the competition among tribes but also by competition among a tribe's male members for females. Yet the appearance of language leads to a struggle of a different kind. As Darwin observes at the beginning of chapter 4, "after the power of language had been acquired, and the wishes of the community could be expressed, the common opinion how each member ought to act for the public good, would naturally become in a paramount degree the guide to action" (472). While an individual might agree with the wishes of the group, at other times he might not, "so that there would often be a struggle as to which impulse should be followed; and satisfaction, dissatisfaction, or even misery would be felt." Torn by conflicting desires, Darwin's ancestor bears a striking resemblance to the middle link, that ancient figure, poetically described by Pope.

> He hangs between; in doubt to act or rest;
> In doubt to deem himself a god or beast.

Darwin's hero may develop by new laws, but as we will see in the next episode, he now faces an age-old dilemma.

CIVILIZATION: in which (8) *the hero is tested again* and by developing his moral sense (9) *triumphs* over lower men and his own lower nature.

As it turns out, the conflict between the individual will and the will of the group also provides Darwin with one of his greatest challenges. The question of morality, Darwin writes at the beginning to chapter 4, "has been discussed by many writers of consummate ability; and my sole excuse for touching on it is the impossibility of here passing it over, and because, as far as I know, no one has approached it exclusively from the side of natural history" (471). Despite the modesty of his approach, Darwin has all along been anticipating his arrival at this question. So carefully has he prepared the way that the evolution of the moral sense appears as a logical consequence of the development of the mental powers and language. "The following proposition seems to me in a high degree probable," Darwin writes, "—namely that any animal whatever, endowed with well-marked social instincts . . . would inevitably acquire a moral sense or conscience, as soon as its intellectual powers had become as well, or nearly as well developed, as in man" (471–72). As soon as the mental faculties had become highly developed, Darwin explains, "images of past actions and motives would be incessantly passing through the brain," providing each individual with a basis for comparing and evaluating his own behavior. Once the power of language had been acquired and "the common opinion how each member ought to act" could be expressed, each individual would be able to compare his performance not only with past acts but also with those prescribed by the community.

Granted high mental powers and a gift for speech, he would not necessarily acquire a conscience, however. The moral sense rests on a prior endowment: well-marked social instincts. In particular, it depends on sympathy, which "forms an essential part of the social instinct, and is indeed its foundation-stone." Although the social instinct is present in other animals, it must have been very strong in man's early ancestors who, to compensate for their comparative weakness, found it advantageous to live in groups. "For with those animals which were benefitted by living in close association, the individuals which took the greatest pleasure in society would best escape various dangers; whilst those that cared least for their comrades would perish in greater numbers" (478).

The social instinct serves the general good of a tribe—for Darwin defines the general good as "the rearing of the greatest number of individuals in full vigour and health, with all their faculties perfect, under the conditions to which they are subjected"—but it does not necessarily raise the moral excellence of a tribe's individual members. The development of the moral sense depends on another and even more powerful stimulus, "namely, the praise and blame of our fellow-men." According to Darwin, man's ability to feel the displeasure of his fellows has been an even greater incentive to moral behavior than his feelings of pleasure in society. "At how early a period the progenitors of man . . . became capable of feeling and being impelled by the praise or blame of their fellow-creatures, we cannot, of course, say" (499). But even dogs and the "rudest savages" feel the sentiments of shame and glory, Darwin reasons. "We may therefore conclude that primeval man, at a very remote period, would have been influenced by the praise and blame of his fellows" (500).

What distinguishes man from dog—and furthers his moral development—is his ability to approve or disapprove of his own behavior and, on that basis, to choose his own actions. Again, this is what isolates the middle-link from the rest of creation. A moral being, Darwin affirms, "is one who is capable of comparing his past and future actions or motives, and of approving or disapproving of them. We have no reason to suppose that any of the lower animals have this capacity." A dog may face danger to aid his master or rescue a child, but he does not choose or reflect on his behavior. A human, on the other hand, will often deliberate before risking his life—with the knowledge that he may suffer guilt for his nonmoral actions.

It is man's ability to choose his actions in light of their consequences that, for Darwin, is "the main point, on which the whole question of the moral sense hinges. Why should a man feel that he ought to obey one instinctive desire rather than another? Why does he bitterly regret if he has yielded to the strong sense of self-preservation, and has not risked his life to save that of a fellow-creature; or why does he regret having stolen food from severe hunger?" (481). Man has greater control over his acts, but he is motivated to a far greater degree than other animals by the promise of reward and punishment. He is, in this regard, as conditioned as Pavlov's dog. So carefully does he pair action with result that, in time, his responses become automatic. "Man prompted by his conscience, will through long habit acquire such perfect self-command, that his desires and passions will at last yield instantly to and without a struggle to his social sympathies" (486).

At this point, when "the more enduring Social Instincts conquer the less Persistent Instincts"—"he will feel himself impelled, independently of any pleasure or pain felt at the moment, to certain lines of conduct. He may then say, I am the supreme judge of my own conduct, and in the words of Kant, I will not in my own person violate the dignity of humanity" (481).

Man may be his own judge and yet he remains a prisoner: "In order to be quite free from self-reproach . . . it is almost necessary for him to avoid the disapprobation, whether reasonable or not, of his fellow men. . . . He must likewise avoid the reprobation of the one-God or gods, in whom according to his knowledge or superstition he may believe; but in this case the additional fear of divine punishment often supervenes" (486–87). Man's hands "act in obedience to his will," but his will obeys that of the larger community. Yet, even the will of the group acts in service to a higher power, the principle of natural selection. As Darwin defines it, the common good is "the rearing of the greatest number of individuals under the conditions to which they are subjected." Man's moral sense, which impels him to do good, develops in accord with the principle of natural selection. "A tribe including members who, from possessing in a high degree the spirit of patriotism, fidelity, obedience, courage and sympathy were always ready to aid one another, and to sacrifice themselves for the common good, would be victorious over most other tribes; and this would be natural selection" (500). Man's moral sense may grow out of the struggle between the lower and higher impulses within men, but it is by the competition of tribe with tribe that it is raised and extends through the species. "A tribe possessing the above qualities in a high degree would spread and be victorious over other tribes; but in the course of time it would, judging from all past history, be in its turn overcome by some other and still more highly endowed tribe" (500). The problem of morality is resolved, like the problem of intelligence, not in man's inner sanctum but on the battlefield.

So too the problem of religion might be explained: belief in "the one-God or gods"—for whom millions have lost their lives—acts in service to the almighty principle of natural selection. Darwin himself serves the cause in his capacity as a disinterested scholar: "The presence of a body of well-instructed men, who have not to labour for their daily bread, is important to a degree which cannot be over-estimated; as all high intellectual work is carried on by them, and on such work material progress of all kinds mainly depends, not to mention other and higher advantages" (502). Darwin appears, like Hitchcock in one of his films, glimpsed in a crowd—"a body of well-instructed men." He inserts himself at an ominous point, under the heading "Natural Selection as affecting Civilised Nations," when good is about to turn evil.

Man's moral sense is acquired gradually according to natural law. As successful tribes expand and competition from other tribes decreases, the principle of natural selection relaxes its grip. Moral practices fall more and more under human jurisdiction. "The judgment of the community will generally be guided by some rude experience of what is best in the long run for all the members; but this judgment will not rarely err from ignorance and weak reasoning. Hence the strangest customs and superstitions, in complete opposition to the true welfare and happiness of mankind, have become all-powerful throughout the world" (491). The caste system, primogeniture, celibacy, infanticide—Darwin enumerates a whole series of "savage" customs. The most dangerous, however, are those practiced by civilized peoples. "We civilised men," Darwin remarks, "do our utmost to check the process of elimination; we build asylums for the imbecile, the maimed, and the sick; we institute poor laws; and our medical men exert their utmost skill to save the life of every one to the last moment. . . . Thus the weak members of civilised societies propagate their own kind. No one who has attended to the breeding of domestic animals will doubt that this must be highly injurious to the race of man" (501). Doctors may alleviate the suffering of individual men, but they do great injury to the species. They check the process of elimination without regard for the basic Darwinian tenet: saving lives is good from an evolutionary point of view only if it allows other lives to be ended.

This fact, that what acts for the good of man within the confines of the tribe may do harm in civilized society, was for Huxley modern man's greatest dilemma. In the "Prolegomena" (1894) to his famous essay "Evolution and Ethics," Huxley compares civilization to a walled garden, set off from the state of nature. "Even should the whole human race be absorbed in one vast polity," Huxley concludes,

> the struggle for existence with the state of nature outside it, and the tendency to the return of the struggle within, in consequence of over-multiplication, will remain; and, unless men's inheritance from the ancestors who fought a good fight in the state of nature, their dose of original sin, is rooted out by some method at present unrevealed, . . . every child born into the world will still bring with him the instinct of unlimited self-assertion. He will have to learn the lesson of self-restraint and renunciation. (1894, 43–44)

Huxley was not optimistic. Darwin had already observed in *The Descent of Man* that the lesson of self-restraint would be most usefully followed by those least likely to practice it: "namely the weaker and inferior members of society."

"Looking to future generations, there is no cause to fear," Darwin predicts; "the struggle between our higher and lower impulses will be less severe, and virtue will be triumphant." Yet Darwin was aware that humans could face a tragic ending rather than a happy one. The real tragedy is that our downfall may lie not in hubris —the "pride and arrogance which made our forefathers declare that they were descended from demigods"—but in sympathy, the "noblest part of our nature." There is one last hope, however. Although sympathy may prove to be man's tragic flaw, it could still save us if used with a proper sense of balance—a sense which Darwin himself demonstrates in telling the story of human evolution. Darwin appeals to our sympathy for the lower animals throughout *The Descent of Man*, but he does so by reinforcing the reader's antipathy for "savages" and the "weaker and inferior members of society." Darwin concludes, as Huxley answered Wilberforce, by preferring a monkey ancestor to a human one.

> For my own part I would as soon be descended from that heroic little monkey, who braved his dreaded enemy in order to save the life of his keeper; or from that old baboon, who, descending from the mountains, carried away in triumph his young comrade from a crowd of astonished dogs—as from a savage who delights to torture his enemies, offers up bloody sacrifices, practises infanticide without remorse, treats his wives like slaves, knows no decency, and is haunted by the grossest superstitions. (919–20)

Darwin elevates the monkey at the savage's expense in order to convert us to his naturalistic point of view and to further human evolution. Emphasizing the differences between savages and civilized men, Darwin instills a kind of chauvinism which is intended to provide an incentive for further moral advancement. It is clear that if it were not for civilized people, Darwin's story would have no living human heroes. Next to savages who are cruel and false, the European appears kindest and most faithful.

It may seem capricious to compare *The Descent of Man* to the story of Cinderella. Yet as Bruno Bettelheim observes in *The Uses of Enchantment*, "'Cinderella' is the best-known fairy tale, and probably also the best-liked" (1977, 236). It is the archetypal rags-to-riches tale: it tells of "the humble being elevated, of true merit being recognized even when hidden under rags, of virtue rewarded and evil punished. . . . But under this overt content is concealed a welter of complex and largely unconscious material, which details of the story allude to just enough to set our unconscious associations going" (1977, 239). According to Bettelheim, one of the morals of the Cinderella tale is the lesson of humility, for it is only by experiencing degradation that we can achieve true glory. Though the details of *The Descent of Man* differ greatly from those of the Cinderella tale, the moral is not very different. "Man may be excused for feeling some pride at having risen, though not through his own exertions to the very summit of the organic scale; and the fact of his having risen, instead of having been aboriginally placed there, may give him hopes for a still higher destiny in the distant future. But . . . we must acknowledge, as it seems to me, that man with all his noble qualities . . . still bears in his bodily frame the indelible stamp of his lowly origin" (405).

Part II

Twentieth-Century Images

 ARTHUR KEITH was five years old when *The Descent of Man* appeared in 1871. Like his great rival Grafton Elliot Smith, he belonged to the first generation that could have read Darwin's book soon after growing out of fairy tales. It was not until medical school that Keith studied *The Descent of Man*, but from then on he considered himself a disciple. Keith recalled Darwin's teachings many times during his scientific career, notably in his 1927 presidential speech to the British Association for the Advancement of Science. "Fifty-five years have come and gone since Charles Darwin wrote a history of man's descent," he began. "An enormous body of new evidence has poured in upon us. We are now able to fill in many pages which Darwin had perforce to leave blank, and we have found it necessary to alter details in his narrative, but the fundamentals of Darwin's outlook of man's history remain unshaken. Nay, so strong has his position become that I am convinced that it never can be shaken" (1927, 203).

Keith himself had filled many pages describing the new evidence discovered in those years, including the remains of *Pithecanthropus* from Java, the Neanderthals and Cro-Magnons from Europe, and the recently unearthed fragments from Piltdown. Keith began his famous book *The Antiquity of Man* (1915) primarily to defend his reconstruction of the Piltdown skull against the interpretation put forth by Elliot Smith of this famous discovery.

But now a different set of findings was being unearthed—in the laboratories of experimental scientists. "With such sources of knowledge being ever extended," Keith predicted, "man will be able in due time not only to write his own history but to explain how and why events took the course they did." Fossil discoveries might demonstrate the steps by which humans had evolved, but Keith was convinced that the experimental study of living organisms would reveal a greater secret: the actual mechanism of human evolution. "If we are to understand the machinery which underlies the evolution of man and ape, we have to enter the factories where they are produced —look within the womb and see the ovum being transformed into an embryo, the embryo into a foetus and the foetus into a babe. . . . When we have discovered the machinery of development and of growth we shall also know the machinery of evolution, for they are the same" (207). Despite his faith in Darwin's story of man's ascent, Keith appears here a disciple of a non-Darwinian theory: the machinery of evolution will be found inside the "factory" of the womb rather than in the mechanism of natural selection.

Natural selection was, in fact, the subject of widespread evolutionary debate during the early twentieth century—a debate even more widespread and heated than the controversy over Piltdown. As Peter Bowler has recently observed, "Non-Darwinian mechanisms such as Lamarckism and orthogenesis were widely accepted by biologists" (1986, 41). Though Keith and Elliot Smith were vehemently opposed to Lamarckism, they were both orthogenists: they believed that the primary evolutionary force lay inside the organism, in the mechanisms by which variations were produced, rather than in the principle of natural selection. Darwin himself had discussed the laws of variation under several heads—"the direct and definite action of changed conditions," "effects of the increased use and disuse of parts," "arrests of development"—but the majority are external causes operating in an opportunistic fashion. "With respect to the causes of variability we are in all cases very ignorant; but we can see that in man as in the lower animals, they stand in some relation to the conditions to which each species has been exposed during several generations" (1971/1948, 111).

Keith, on the other hand, believed that structural variations were largely the result of internal forces operating along predetermined lines: "The machinery of evolution works out its untrammelled ends in the embryo and the foetus" (1923a, 268). Elliot Smith also believed evolution to be directed by an internal factor: "the steady and uniform development of the brain along a well-defined course . . . must give us the fundamental reason for 'man's emergence and ascent,' whatever other factors may contribute toward that consummation" (1924, 20).

Despite the declaration of faith in Keith's 1927 presidential address, the fundamentals of Darwin's outlook on human evolution —the creative role of natural selection—were not upheld by either of these two main British proponents of human evolution. As this section will show, Keith and Elliot Smith altered not only the details of Darwin's narrative of human evolution but also the fundamental principles. Keith put bipedalism first and Elliot Smith, the brain, but both conceived of human evolution as a story in which internal factors act as the creative force or "donor." Though natural selection does play a role, it is not the role conceived by Darwin: it operates primarily by eliciting variations rather than selecting among those individuals who already possess them.

Darwin did not present his story of human evolution from beginning to end; nor do the narratives of Keith and Elliot Smith appear in one continuous sequence or even in one treatise. They must be pieced together from narrative fragments in books and articles published between 1890 and 1930. Even if these individual writings lack the artistic unity of literary works, recurring images and metaphors can be seen in the collected works of Elliot Smith and Keith, as in the oeuvre of an author. The images of Keith's "womb" and Elliot Smith's "tomb" highlight each scientist's unique vision of human evolution, for as I will show, Keith's donor works its ends in the embryo and the foetus, whereas Elliot Smith's donor resides in the skull vault. Although my primary purpose is to reconstruct the stories of Keith and Elliot Smith, I try also to show how these stories developed over the courses of their careers. Each chapter begins with a brief biographical sketch, highlighting the formative influence of early training on the overall conception of human evolution and on the interpretation of specific fossils. The Piltdown controversy is the occasion for the confrontation between Keith and Elliot Smith, but their debate over this fossil skull is insignificant compared to the profound difference in their interpretations of the primary cause, or donor, of human evolution.

4 Keith's Womb

EITH'S story of human evolution tells of a lazy son, but his own autobiography speaks of one who has toiled. "If after death any image is found engraven on my brain, I am sure it will prove to be that of a human skull. The days I have spent—I almost wrote, wasted—in seeking to wrest from it secrets concerning human evolution are beyond number" (1950, 341). That "almost . . . wasted" is prophetic—and poignant. In 1953 the Piltdown hoax was exposed, revealing to the eighty-seven-year-old Keith, who had wrestled with human skulls in order to interpret the find, that he had squandered even more than he reckoned.

From the start of his career, Keith was aware of the dangers of studying human evolution. "Only four individuals to represent the millions and millions of men that must have lived and died in Quaternary times!" (1895c, 354), Keith exclaimed in his first paper on fossil man. Of all the human fossils then known, the German Neanderthal skull, the skull cap of *Pithecanthropus* from Java, and two Belgian skulls (later identified as Cro-Magnon) were complete enough for the purposes of reconstruction. Even these fossils were of limited value: "for the purposes of giving us a clue to the human line of descent, the fossil remains at present known assist us not one single jot" (369). Keith did not publish another word on fossil man for more than a decade.

To begin, living organisms occupied Keith more than did fossils. Apart from his 1895 fossil review, his early publications are anatomical studies of living primates based on dissections made while he was a medical officer to a Siamese mining concession (1889–92). Keith's jungle studies bore much fruit; they provided the starting point for his famous set of lectures on the evolution of the human posture (1923b). More immediately, they revealed the abundant anatomical variation exhibited within species of monkeys, apes, and humans: "When brains of individuals of any species of ape whatsoever are set side by side, a very considerable degree of variation in size is manifested. This fact countenances the conception that the brain-masses which characterise the Catarrhine genera are only individual variations accumulated and cemented by Selection" (1895a, 282). In describing selection as a "cementing" rather than a creative force, Keith foreshadows his non-Darwinian views. These beliefs are also evident in the conclusions to a paper written the same year on the variations exhibited by the carotid and subclavian arteries. "A type has rightly come to be recognised as a mental realisation with no bone and flesh embodiment; . . . the race becomes, as it were, a great amoeboid form, with its preponderating variations thrown out as pseudopodia feeling towards adaptation" (1895b, 457).

Years later, Keith would describe how adaptations are established by the groping of flanks of cells, actively reaching like pseudopodia. His later beliefs are prefigured in a final metaphor. "If the theory of descent be true . . . we may regard the animals that, structurally, most nearly approximate to Man as control experiments launched by Nature, upon which we may test our speculations as to the causes of human variation" (456). As we will see, Keith would pursue the search for the laws by which human variations are generated almost to the point of ignoring the part played by natural selection in shaping "Nature's experiments."

Keith's first laboratory was the jungles of Siam. His professional post for most of his career was Conservator of the Museum of the

Royal College of Surgeons in London. Keith moved to the museum in 1908, the same year that the Neandertal of Le Moustier and the Cro-Magnon man of La Chapelle were discovered. Keith was once again dismayed by the fossil record, though for a different reason. "Everyone starts away in life with the conviction that the evolution of man is a recent event and must have proceeded in orderly sequence from a lower stage to a higher. There can be no doubt that the Neanderthal type is lower than the modern type of man. It was expected that the Neanderthal type would disappear and be succeeded by the modern type" (1912, 734). Yet the French Neanderthal remains appeared to be more recent than the fossils of modern men recently found in England at Ipswich, Galley Hill, and Dartford. They demonstrated that Neanderthals evolved *after* modern humans.

Though the chronology of the Neanderthals was subsequently revised, Keith learned from these discoveries two central lessons which became cornerstones of his views on human evolution: humans had existed relatively unchanged over long periods of time; and human evolution had worked in a "disorderly" way—not in a progressive sequence. The first is announced in the title of his classic, *The Antiquity of Man* (1915), while the second is reflected in the opening paragraph to its prototype, *Ancient Types of Man* (1911).

> As I sit down to write the story of the various forms which the body of man has assumed in ancient times, I find it difficult to determine whether I should begin at the beginning or at the end. Were the story now complete, there would be no difficulty: it should be told from the beginning. Some day, no doubt, it will be told thus, but at present the known phases of man's early history are so few, so fragmentary and so isolated, that a survey of the later and better known phases is needed to place the earlier stages in their proper perspective. For that reason, I propose to reverse the usual order, and trace man's physical history from the present into the far past. (1911, 1)

Keith may have been inspired also by his recent tour (1910) of the French Neanderthal sites, for his book reads like a Baedeker of human evolution. We begin not at a point in the remote past but on the modern day coast of Essex, where the sea "washes against a flat coast-line, cutting and exposing on the beach remains of a buried or prehistoric floor" (1−2). Similarly, *The Antiquity of Man* opens on the road from London to Maidstone.

> The traveller along this road, with his face turned eastwards, be he ever so interested in the study of ancient man, cannot fail to note the picturesqueness of the Kentish weald. From time to time he passes villages which have preserved, in spite of a whirling stream of motor traffic, much of an old-world atmosphere. . . . Here and there he may trace the Pilgrim's Way as it winds along the foot of the steep grey face of the Downs, the mediaeval path to the shrine at Canterbury. (1915, 1)

Compared to Huxley's cosmic descent, this pilgrimage is a country stroll, and its purpose is more limited. Whereas Huxley brings his awe-struck traveler to the realization that he has evolved, Keith leads him away from a Darwinian perspective to a new view of the mechanics of evolution.

"We expected to find evolution working in an orderly manner, passing step by step from a Simian to a modern type of man," Keith had written in *Ancient Types of Man*. "It will be seen, however, that the succession of human races is disorderly, and that the race which survives is not necessarily the one with the big body or with the big brain, nor even that in which there is a combination of such characters" (1911, 27). In *The Antiquity of Man*, the Darwinian view is even more disorienting. "We are naturally astonished to find that men who have preceded us so long ago—men of a former geologic epoch—should so far outstrip their successors of to-day who regard themselves as 'the survival of the fittest,' and believe the fittest to be the race with the biggest brains. We cannot quarrel with the facts but how are we to explain them?" (1915, 54).

Keith had in fact found an answer several years before in Bayliss and Starling's 1905 discovery of hormones. Compared to his earlier recounting of fossil finds, this discovery is a much more exciting journey. "Up to that time we had been like an outlandish visitor to a strange city, who believed that the visible telegraph or telephone wires were the only means of communication between its inhabitants. We believed that it was only by nerve-fibres that intercommunication was established in the animal body. Bayliss and Starling showed that there was a postal system" (1919, 304–05). Keith discovered Starling's work in 1908, the same year as the Le Moustier Neanderthal find. The following year, he made a connection between the discoveries. Sitting in front of a museum case in which a cast of a Neanderthal skull and the skull of a human acromegalic were exhibited side by side, he was struck by the similarities. Thanks to Starling's work, Keith knew that acromegaly was due to an excess of pituitary hormone. "The peculiar characters of the Neanderthal type appear to be under the particular domination of the small pituitary gland at the base of the brain. When this gland becomes enlarged, as it occasionally does in the disease known as acromegaly, the Neanderthal characters are developed in the subjects of the disease in an exaggerated and bizarre form. The functions of the pituitary seem to afford a key to Neanderthal characteristics" (1911, 120).

The study of growth disorders offered a clue to the puzzle of "disorderliness" in human evolution. In the same manner that "growth disorders—dwarfism and giantism—are but derangements of the normal machinery of growth" (1923a, 264), evolutionary disorders—such as the appearance of bizarre species—were derangements of a normal evolutionary process. Keith's next challenge was to discover the mechanism by which normal "adaptations" arose: the machinery of evolution. Once again, he turned excitedly to experimental science. "Any one who has followed the success with which physicists have unravelled the structure of the atom in recent years will not despair of an equal success attending the efforts of embryologists to uncover the means by which one group of embryonic cells regulates the growth of a neighbouring group" (260). Like the atom, the embryo must be conceived in terms of regulatory forces rather than structures.

Keith immediately applied this insight to the study of evolution: "The evolutionary machinery lies in the behaviour of the embryonic cell." The study of the eye had already shown how "one group of living cells can enslave and control the behaviour of another group." Similarly, the brain might have developed through control and domination. "If we conceive of a mob of war-seasoned men to deploy automatically and to take up effective battle-stations we have before us a picture of what is to be seen taking place among the nerve cells in the brain of the growing human embryo" (260). Yet battlefields become messy places once the action begins: mistakes are made and lives are lost, whereas nothing fails in the embryonic regiment.

> The success with which the developing muscle cells reach their ultimate destinations is one of surprising accuracy; they may take hold of a spine or a rib too far up or too low down, but the total result is always one which makes the whole muscle into an effective mechanical engine. . . . In these variations of attachment we are seeing evolution at work, and its machinery lies in the forces which regulate or control the migratory movements of the young muscle cells. (261)

Keith describes the embryo as a flawless machine, yet he evokes here an earlier organic metaphor. The image of flanks of muscle cells climbing "too far up or too far down" is reminiscent of his 1895 description of variations as "pseudopodia feeling towards adaptation." Keith actually compares embryonic tissues to protozoa in his 1923 Huxley Lecture: "The embryonic cells retain many of the purposive, almost conscious, attributes possessed by primitive unicellular organisms. No doubt the behaviour of embryonic cells, as of the simplest protozoa, will prove to be reflex in nature—mere protoplasmic responses to appropriate stimuli" (268). Keith undertook this lecture to demonstrate that adaptations arose "not by the working of any selective law but in powers which were resident in living, developing tissues." He emphasizes this point with yet another metaphor:

> To make my meaning clear, let me borrow a simile from human affairs. Some thirty years ago, in the incipient stages which led to the modern development of the great motor-car industry, small

workshops sprang up in almost every town and supplied a car of local design for local needs. The struggle for survival set in, and successful types, ousting local types, led to the formation of great firms which catered for the needs of continents. The workmen engaged and the types of car made became specialised and standardised. These great firms, we know, keep an eye on the market—benefit by experience—and modify their types to suit demand. Invention succeeds invention in their workshops. But in the factory where human types of body and mind are produced I am presuming there is no intelligence department. . . . All hands in the human factory are co-ordinated—not by orders from managers or foremen, but by a self-regulating system of hormone-control which works out functional ends automatically. (268)

This theme reappears in his 1927 presidential address to the British Association for the Advancement of Science. Although Keith claims there to uphold "the fundamentals of Darwin's outlook on man's history," his factory simile—with its emphasis on the internal control of production—contradicts the essence of Darwin's theory of evolution: the creative role of natural selection. Keith's metaphor depicts a highly efficient process resulting in the production of fully formed adaptations, whereas in the Darwinian view, evolution is a highly wasteful process in which adaptations are shaped through the elimination of unfit variants. In this sense, Keith's image of the cooly efficient womb presents a significant contrast to what Gould has described as a central image of Darwin's view of nature: the bloody "hecatomb" or great sacrifice.

Keith's belief that the locus of evolution lies in the embryo had further implications: adaptations arise by the retention of fetal characteristics. "We need not be surprised, seeing how plastic and resourceful the embryonic tissues are, to find most—but not all—of man's characteristic features appear in a modified form as transitional phases in the foetal stages of man's nearest allies—the anthropoid apes." Humans retain the fetal characters of their ape-like ancestors rather than recapitulating their adult traits, as Haeckel believed. This principle, named Bolk's Law after its embryologist-discoverer, offers a key for "a true interpretation to such human features as are represented by man's small face and jaws; his forehead tending to be devoid of supraorbital ridges, his large head poised on a long and relatively slender neck: they are features first produced in the foetal stages of higher primates and now retained by man in his adult state" (268).

Even the human brain obeys Bolk's Law, for as we will see, it attains prominence in Keith's narrative by retaining into adolescence the rapid rates of growth found in the fetus. Indeed, the true end of human evolution, according to Keith, is to recreate in the human adult all the qualities of the embryo.

> In man the evolutionary tendency has been to retain more and more the structural characters of youth; in the gorilla the tendency has been in the opposite direction—to increase the size of the jaw and strength of body. In his evolutionary career man has moved in the direction of the brain, while his cousin the gorilla has moved in the direction of brawn. The evolutionary process which has produced such diverse forms from a common ancestor constitutes at once the most enigmatic and also the most interesting experiment to be found in the whole realm of Nature. (1926, 491)

Keith's metaphor of "Nature's experiment" is more refined here than in his 1895 passage. If the process of fetalization is under hormonal control, as Keith believed it to be, then nature has produced the differences between humans and apes as she might in the lab: by manipulating their hormone levels.

Keith attaches his understanding of human evolution to fossil skulls, and yet he interprets fossils, in large part, by assessing the extent to which they retain embryonic proportions. In the following pages we will see how Keith's faith in the tenets of physiology affects the presentation of fossils in his narrative of human evolution.

ARBOREALITY: in which (1) *the scene is set* in the jungles of Siam, and (2) *the hero is introduced*, orthograde and gibbonish.

Keith's story of human evolution could begin like a true adventure tale—with a glimpse of our ancestors through parted jungle branches. "The first time I saw them make a hurried departure I was filled with amazement. They swung themselves by their arms, hand over hand, keeping their bodies upright, and using their feet for support as they sped along. The impetus which carried them in their daring leaps from tree to tree was obtained by an arm-swing" (1950, 121). Keith's autobiographical recollections of the gibbons in the jungles of Siam offer a fanciful view of man's ancestors at our story's start. His famous 1923 lectures "Man's Posture: Its Evolution and Disorders" provide a scientific rationale for his choice of the gibbon as early protagonist. There Keith recounts the results of his early dissections: "In their arrangement the bones and muscles of the gibbon were altogether human while the same parts of the semnopitheque and macaque which outwardly looked like they might be cousins to the gibbon were different. It was then that I realized that the history of many of man's postural adaptations had to be traced back to the anatomy of the gibbonish or hylobatian body" (1925, 452).

In his observations of their movements, Keith was further struck by the differences between the gibbons and the Asian monkeys *Semnopithecus* and *Macacus*.

In his flight from tree to tree the gibbon's manner of progression differs . . . from that of monkeys. It is true that before starting flight the resting posture of gibbon and monkey are the same; both sit in a semi-erect posture, resting on ischial callosities. In progression the gibbon uses his arms as the chief means of support and of propulsion as he leaps with his arms; the lower limbs are defined as accessory means of support or as the chief means of running along horizontal branches. . . . The semnopitheque was a heavy jumper in whose forward leap the impetus came from the hinder limbs and loins; the hands and arms were used to clutch the branches . . . but were never used in the hand-over-

hand manner which is habitual in the gibbon—a true trapeze
artist. (1923b, 453)

Like Huxley, Keith concluded that the morphological and behavioral differences between monkeys and apes were greater than those
which existed between apes and humans: "So far as concerns the
group of primates to which man belongs we may safely say that the
great structural revolution which marks [their] history . . . occurred
with the evolution of the gibbon. It is to this . . . structural revolution that man owes the chief of his postural modifications" (453).[1]

Keith's opening glimpse of a gibbon flying through the trees is
but a distant view. The real focus will be on the anatomy and physiology of the gibbonlike protagonist, rather than his habitat and
behavior. "With the evolution of the upright or orthograde spine
there took place a shortening of the lumbar part of the spinal column"; "With a headward sacralization there is also a forward movement of the sacral and lumbar plexuses, although the forward shift
of the nerves lags slightly behind that of the vertebrae." The evolution of the upright posture entails the coordinated movements of
more than just the muscles, nerves, and bones. "Ribs, vertebrae,
sternum, body wall and spinal muscles, diaphragm, pleurae, lungs
and heart underwent a simultaneous and harmonious adaptational
transformation. To account for such a structural revolution we
must postulate a much more elaborate mechanism controlling
developmental processes than any we have a knowledge of as yet"
(454).

The donor, in the guise of a controlling mechanism, is still a
mysterious figure at this early stage in Keith's narrative. For the moment, Keith's detailed anatomical description may be used to pre-

---

1. Keith had first expressed these views in 1903 in the form of a "working
hypothesis." "The Primates [are] divided into two very distinct groups—those which
carry the axis of the body in a horizontal position—the *Pronograde Primates*, including the cynomorphous apes of the Eastern and Western hemispheres; and those which
carry the axis of the body in an upright position—the *Orthograde Primates*, into
which group fall the gibbon, chimpanzee, gorilla and man. The pronograde primate
is certainly the earlier type; from it the orthograde was evolved, probably near the
commencement of the Miocene Period. The earliest type of the orthograde primate
of which we have any knowledge is the gibbon" (1903, 18–19).

sent the hero and also to set the scene: the real action will unfold inside the hero's body rather than in the jungle.

Though no fossil represents the hero at this stage, Keith uses the remains of *Propliopithecus*, a gibbonlike fossil ape, to fix on a date and a possible location for the beginning of his story. "That the orthograde gibbon type had been differentiated from the pronograde monkey type at an early period is proved by the discovery of the remains of fossil apes in the Oligocene . . . of Egypt, which in point of geological age are intermediate to the older Eocene and more recent Miocene formations" (453). So Keith's narrative starts once upon a time in the Oligocene, which according to the geological time scale then in use began three million years before the present.[2]

BIPEDALISM: in which (3) *the situation changes* and "man, by what means we know not, became adapted to plantigrade progression."

The remote ancestor was a gibbonish form, but it did not give rise to humans directly: "From the Hylobatian (gibbon) type of orthograde primate have sprung what may be named—for temporary purposes—the *giant primates*, of which type the orang, the chimpanzee, gorilla, and man are the present-day representatives" (1903, 19). This transition is fleshed out in Keith's 1923 lectures. "With the evolution of the great anthropoids from the small, the weight of the body undergoing then an eight- or twelve-fold increase, adaptations for the orthograde posture and gait were necessarily modified as well as strengthened" (1923b, 453). The giant stage entails a lengthening of the hindlimbs relative to the arms, although it is unclear what adaptive function is served by this change in limb proportions. Keith does not describe how this giant primate moved in the trees. Nor does he offer an adaptive explanation for the increase in size, which appears to be unsuited to an arboreal existence. Keith leaves us hanging on this point. In effect, the hero appears to be a large ape

2. The Oligocene is now established to have begun 36 million years ago.

holding on to a hylobatian existence. "The real change comes after the giant stage: In the evolution of the human stock from that of the arboreal giant primates, [another] stage must be recognized whereby man, by what means we know not, became adapted to plantigrade progression" (1903, 19).

As Keith clarifies, the plantigrade "is the really human stage . . . when the line leading on to man branched off from the great anthropoid stock." Though Keith does not say so, this branching off is probably a consequence of the migration of muscles and bones rather than a move from arboreal to terrestrial (or at least it is contingent upon anatomical changes associated with the plantigrade posture). Keith describes how the loins are lengthened, the rib cage shortened, and the pelvic base enlarged. "With each step toward the plantigrade posture of man, there must have been further specializations in the reflex centres which control the distribution of blood and in the structures which support the weight of the blood mass" (1923b, 454).

In contrast to the orthograde gibbonish phase in which the fore-limbs assumed all the work, now the arms must be supported: "In the climbing, moving arboreal anthropoid the arms and shoulders have to sustain or help to sustain the weight of the trunk, whereas in man the trunk has to sustain the weight of the shoulders and arms" (546). Keith does not refer to the freeing of the hand, as Darwin did, or to any advantage of having the arms suspended. To the contrary, the arms are a burden. Also, whereas the hands are "perfected" before the feet in *The Descent of Man*, the forelimb develops after the hindlimb in Keith's narrative: "The postural mechanism for the maintenance of man's shoulders . . . must have come with the adaptation of his lower limbs as the sole organs of support and progression" (546).

In fact, the plantigrade stage depends primarily on the building up of the lower limbs. "The knees and thighs became more extended and strengthened until the lower limbs came to appear as if they were a downward continuation of the trunk. The pelvis or fulcrum of the lower limbs, as also of the spinal column, was modified; the hip and knee joints became adapted to the new posture; the muscles and bones of the leg assumed a human form; and, above all the foot was transformed" (453). Ultimately the upright posture rests on the building up of the plantar arch, but this structure is a consequence of the development of the nonopposable big toe or hallux:

> Hence it is that, up to a stage corresponding to the point reached by a human embryo at the end of the second month of development, the foot and toes of man and ape are much alike—the toes radiate forwards from the tarsus and all are united in a common web. . . . Then at the stage where the webbing disappears from the digits of the foetal ape and the great toe assumes its separate status, the foot of man goes on retaining the great toe in the primitive adducted embryonic position. (670)

The great toe is due to the retention of a fetal stage, as are other distinctively human structures. "It will be found to be true of nearly all the structural features which are distinctive of man's body that they make their first appearance in the embryonic or foetal stages of apes; subsequently they blossom to their full in man's body. Such foetal structures are not, as so often thought, recapitulations of ancestral phases; they are new evolutionary creations" (670).

Man's distinctive structures originate in the womb not by Haeckel's principle of ontogeny recapitulating phylogeny—by the fetus passing through ancestral states—but by a "blossoming" of fetal stages in the adult. The machinery of human growth operates by letting fetal buds mature along their own course, uncorrupted by the hormonal excess that produces the brutish traits of chimps and gorillas. This flourishing of fetal states is a controlled and conservative process. Structural changes are made, as new factory products might be produced, along "predetermined lines of modification."

> The fact that the most characteristic features of the human body appear first in embryonic or foetal life, and that human-like characters appear transiently in foetal stages of anthropoid apes, the further fact that many constant structural modifications of man's body are seen as occasional variations of the ape's body all bear out Huxley's dictum that evolution tends to evolve along prede-

termined lines of modification. The machinery of evolution works out its untrammelled ends in the embryo. (1923a, 268)

Haeckel—and also Darwin—admitted the possibility that external factors, such as Lamarck's principle of use-disuse, might affect the "perfecting and differentiation" of man's limbs. Keith explicitly omits such unruly neo-Lamarckian factors. "The human foot was never shaped by any effort made by the growing or grown anthropoid ape, as Lamarck supposed, but arose for the first time in the embryonic foot—under the influence of the growth mechanism which controls the development of that organ" (1923b, 670).

Though this mechanism still remains obscure, the active donor role assigned to it is especially marked in contrast to the passive role played by the hero. "Man has come by his great gifts—his brain, his upright posture, his strange foot and his nimble hand—not by any effort of his own, but, like a favoured child of the present day, has fallen heir to a fortune for which he has never laboured" (1923a, 268). Like the archetypal profligate son, Keith's hero has not earned his wealth—and, as we will see, does not always spend it wisely, hence his postural disorders. Nor have his anthropoid forebears struggled to produce this bequest. Man owes his great gifts of body and mind to the millions of cellular operatives toiling inside the embryo under the control of hormones.

Once again, Keith uses the fossil record primarily for the purposes of calibration: "The plantigrade posture was evolved as soon as the common giant stock began to break up into its various living and fossil forms. We know for certain that this stock was in existence before the middle of the Miocene period, and it is therefore prior to that very remote date, most likely about the beginning of the Miocene or end of the Oligocene—two or three millions of years ago at the lowest estimate—that the plantigrade posture began to be evolved" (1923b, 453). *Dryopithecus*, dated at two to three million years old, is a possible ancestor to the apes but anatomically is too primitive to represent the plantigrade stage of evolution. On the other hand, *Pithecanthropus* has a fully human femur but, dated at well under a million years old, is too recent to be cast as the hero. It serves as an exemplar rather than an actual ancestor. "From a survey of this extinct form of man we can draw the important inference that our teeth and our posture were evolved at a stage when our brain, as regards volume and shape, had passed through only the earlier stages of the development which has lifted it above the anthropoid condition" (1911, 140).

With its relatively small brain and human teeth, *Australopithecus*, discovered by Raymond Dart in 1925, might fill the role, but Keith rejects it on the grounds that it is not a well-accredited biped. "Professor Dart . . . leans to the supposition that Australopithecus may have assumed the posture and habits which have become perfected in man, and thus was able to wander far beyond the jungle limits. We cannot be certain of posture until we find a bone of the lower limb. One cannot see any character in the skull which justifies the supposition of the erect posture" (1925e, 326). The forward position of the foramen magnum and the "head balancing index," which Dart adduces as evidence of bipedalism, are not conclusive since, as Keith argues, they could be due to the fact that the only known skull of *Australopithecus* belonged to a juvenile.

"To have any claim to stand in or near the human line of descent [*Australopithecus*] must be able to claim an early Miocene date at least." The Pliocene *Australopithecus* is too recent. It is, in fact, contemporaneous with the much larger brained *Pithecanthropus* and also with Piltdown. Keith's preoccupation with the Piltdown skull colored his thinking about many fossils, almost to the point of self-contradiction: Piltdown, with its human braincase and apelike teeth, contradicts the inference drawn from *Pithecanthropus*—that "our teeth and our posture were evolved at a stage when our brain . . . had passed through only the earlier stages of development"—whereas the rejected *Australopithecus* substantiates this important lesson.

Finally, Keith dismisses *Australopithecus* on paleoecological grounds: "All living anthropoid apes are confined to tropical jungles. The limestone bluff which served as a tomb for this new anthropoid child lies 2,000 miles from the haunts of the gorilla and chimpanzee. The first supposition one makes—and it is justified by what we know of Europe—is that the climate of South Africa has changed, and that the tropical belt had once spread over the deserts of Bechuanaland" (1925e, 326). Keith presumes that the Taungs child made its lair in the jungles as living apes do, despite the fact that it lived thousands of miles from the nearest known ape habitats. On this basis he assumes that jungles once covered the deserts of Southern Africa. In imagining that these tropical forests might turn into deserts in a fraction of the time that it takes to transform the muscles of an anthropoid into those of a man, Keith reveals his essential bias: his inclination to subordinate the workings of the external to the internal landscape.

TERRESTRIALITY: in which, "no longer confined to tracts of tropical jungle," (4) *the hero departs* and begins his "glorious exodus."

Though Keith describes in great detail how the shift to the plantigrade phase occurs, he does not say why—for what adaptive reason—it happened. Unlike Darwin, he does not discuss the advantage of having the hands free; perhaps this is because the hero, having already passed through a giant stage, is not quite as small and defenseless as Darwin's semihuman progenitor. The increase in size might have led him down from the trees, but even that would not be sufficient reason for adopting the upright posture since, as Keith observes, the male gorilla, whose weight compels him to the ground, uses his forelimbs for support and progression. (Again, for Keith, there is no necessary link between the upright posture and terrestriality.)

The descent to the ground is shrouded in mist, but it has clear and important consequences: "Any anthropoid who had acquired the human mode of progression had gained an enormous advantage; it would no longer be confined to tracts of tropical jungle but would have the whole length and breadth of the earth open to it" (1923b, 451). As Keith earlier observed, the human posture enables man to "wander far beyond the jungle limits" in contrast to the apes who are "confined" by their mode of progression. The idea that the descent to the ground signifies a kind of evolutionary escape is found in many paleoanthropological tales (Landau 1987). A related idea is that this act of "rebellion" is ultimately punished. Keith's hero suffers for his recklessness, as we will later see when he seeks a second escape, this time from the "ills of civilization." Nevertheless, the shift to the ground is initially a "glorious exodus": it leads to the "dominion of earth, sea and sky." Yet the terrestrial realm is a rather tame place: there for the taking, like his arboreal inheritance, rather than the conquering. There is little mention of predation, famine, or drought; nor does competition pose a threat at this point in the narrative.

Keith's terrestrial landscape is not entirely free of obstacles, however. Physical barriers "such as the Himalayas, extensive tracts of desert such as the Sahara, and wide seas such as the Atlantic" (1928, 315) play an important role in the story. By blocking free passage, they force man's ancestors to inhabit well-defined territories. Yet this tendency to live in territorial groups is not entirely a response to the obstacles posed by the terrestrial environment: "Anthropoid communities are broken up into small families or troops. There are seasonal migrations which follow the ripening of fruits, shoots, and roots, but each anthropoid community keeps within its own beat" (1925f, 55). Whether man's ancestors are drawn to the ground by the search for new food is unclear. In any case, it may be inferred from Keith's passage that the social habits of these proto-men are a continuation of an earlier trend, rather than a response to the selective pressures of the terrestrial environment.

The terrestrial world is divided, then, into two realms—inside the tribe and outside the tribe. This division sets the scene for the rest of Keith's tale, as in *The Descent of Man*, but with different consequences. According to Keith, the main effect of "the tribal machinery" is to segregate its members rather than, as in Darwin's account, to bring them into competition. "No matter how potent may be the physiological machinery which is at work within a group of people, it cannot work out its full effects unless there is also in operation some system of segregation which causes the members of a group to cling to each other, and which also at the same time serves to isolate its members from all surrounding or competing groups" (1928, 315). As Keith elsewhere describes, the tribe is "one of Nature's evolutionary cradles"—it protects and nurtures the physiological machinery of the embryo. But even the physiological machinery serves a greater creative force. So, the donor reveals herself in the next episode, feminine and ferociously fertile.

CIVILIZATION: in which the *donor* "bends man's instincts to suit her species-building purpose."

Man's intelligence develops within the confines of the tribe, but only after his moral virtues have been cultivated. "There never was a tribe, not even when a simian form was assuming a human shape, that was lawless inside its own territory."

> A tribe could survive only if its members were susceptible to the feelings of vanity and of shame. Shame, vanity, fear, terror, gullibility, idealism, and enthusiasm are all essential parts of the tribal machinery. Tribal opinion secured obedience; ostracism from a tribe was a death sentence. In our present state of ignorance it is useless to seek for the machinery which Nature employed to make man's brain rejoice in the tribal attributes of mercy, charity, sacrifice, and mutual service. (1925f, 45–46)

The hero is blessed, this time by mental gifts, but he is at a disadvantage compared to Darwin's primitive tribesman. Lacking the special quality of inventiveness that was instrumental to the freeing of the hand and the development of upright posture in *The Descent of Man*, he follows his instincts rather than his will: he obeys the laws of the tribe automatically. Indeed, he and his fellows are like cells under the control of hormones. "In the earlier stages of the evolution of human society we see that the machinery of government is represented by the automatic working of a herd-instinct—an instinct tending in all its operations towards the preservation of the community" (1923a, 268).

Despite the supposed freedom entailed by the descent from the trees to the ground, Keith's terrestrial prehuman is a cog in "a double machinery": "(1) a physiological machinery, mainly endocrine in nature, which determines the growth and characterization of the body; (2) a psychological machinery which lies at the very root of human mentality" (1928, 316). Implanted in man's brain, the psychological machinery functions to isolate the tribe and hence "to preserve the 'cradle' in which the physiological forces are in operation." But both of these machineries—the physiological and psychological—serve a greater cause: the production of new species. "Tribal organization provides the machinery of isolation or segregation which is necessary if physiological processes are to work towards a new racial type. . . . The brain of man was evolved under tribal conditions; its faculties, its feelings, emotions, and reactions are adapted to serve the needs of tribal organization. Incidentally, they serve the cause of evolutionary progress by producing the effects of isolation or segregation" (315). The tension between unmotivated automatism—the "self-regulating system of hormone control which works out functional ends automatically"—and purposiveness, which has been building up, emerges more clearly at this point. Evolutionary progress, or the production of species, is more than an "incidental" cause. It is nature's final purpose.

> Nature is jealous of her art of species building. Progress—or what is the same thing, Evolution—is her religion; the production of new species is her form of worship. She is up to every trick in this game she plays with living things. There is no artifice or device, however ingenious it may be, which she will not resort to if her end can thus be gained. No mother ever nursed her baby more watchfully and fondly than she does her incipient species. Above all she tries to isolate them to keep them from contamination, just as jealously as a breeder does his herds, flock and fowl runs. She even moulds the brain of man and bends his instincts to suit her species-building purposes (1925f, 42–43).

So the donor of Keith's narrative finally appears, though she has been pulling the strings all along. In contrast with this manipulative fertility goddess, the hero appears truly puppetlike. His raison d'etre is to be a new species. "We human beings are the subjects of her experiment—the pawns of her great game. She sacrifices without compunction in order to win her game. It is here that the religion of the Darwinist comes to his aid: it helps him to understand the apparent injustices of the game of life. Not that his religion is one of pure resignation. He watches Nature at play to learn if it be possible to modify the rules of her game. He learns and hopes to accomplish his object" (71–72).

Keith, the Darwinist, appears in his own narrative as Nature's pupil. Yet he studies nature as he might study a woman's ways, with the desire to domesticate her. For nature is a cruel goddess who uses men to advance her own purposes. She grants the hero favors—gifts of body and mind—not to help him in his journey but for her own ends: the production of new species. It is toward this end that she will finally grant man his greatest gift, the power of reason, in the next episode. Though initially he will use it on nature's behalf, to devise new ways to protect the tribe, reason gives man access to nature's own power of creation. By learning her ways—by building machinery and factories of his own—Keith's hero struggles to undo "Nature's handiwork."

Yet, as we will see, Keith's hope that man may "smash the evolutionary machinery" is even less likely than Darwin's expectation that "virtue will be triumphant over his lower impulses." Reason is granted too late in Keith's account; by the time it appears, man is more than half manufactured. If he were to "smash" the evolutionary machinery, he would destroy the greater part of his brain and body.

ENCEPHALIZATION: in which (5) *the hero is tested* in the "battlefields" of his mind and by means of Reason—(6) *the donor's gift*—is (7) *transformed* into a being who "may be called human."

With the appearance of reason the transformation to humanity occurs. Though upright and tribal, until they acquire reason man's ancestors are, like the apes, "slaves to their instincts, feelings and emotions—the wolves and jackals which occupy the kennels of the inner apartment of their low mentality. Reason has not yet appeared in the subconscious vaults of the brain to tame its wild denizens" (56). A brain without reason is a low and disorderly place. The metaphors which Keith uses to describe the rational mind—"a system of government," "a vast community"—are very similar to those he applies to the embryo. Reason seems to function in the brain as hormones do inside the womb: as a means of order, control, and harmony. As Keith makes clear, this magical double-edged sword has been the hero's greatest tool in his struggle to become human. "Nor should there be any doubt as to the battlefield wherein man has won, and is winning, his victories. The battle is being fought within himself; reason has been struggling for dominion in the fields of his consciousness" (64).

Considering the inner turmoil it later incurs, the granting of reason does appear a capricious act of nature. Unlike Darwin's semihuman progenitors, Keith's prehumans can survive in a group in an almost mindless state. Perhaps this is why Keith calls human evolution nature's greatest experiment; it has no other purpose than to try something different. The appearance of reason is odd in another way: unlike the moral attributes which build upon instincts and feelings inherited from the anthropoid apes, reason is a new addition. "Before [reason] could appear in such humble surroundings upper storeys had to be added to the anthropoid brain, storeys which serve as treasuries of memory and judgment. It was this addition which converted the anthropoid brain into one which may be called human. How this conversion came about—how these upper storeys came to be added—we do not know, but the problem is not insoluble" (57).

A possible clue to this problem lies in one of Keith's earliest scientific papers, "Growth of brain in men and monkeys, with a short criticism of the usual method of starting brain-ratios" (1895a). (It was there that Keith first described selection as a "cementing force.") The main purpose of this paper was to investigate physiological rates of growth rather than evolutionary principles.

The point which specifically interested me was this: The rates at which the brain and the spinal cord grow are quite different; the brain begins with a rush of growth and then slows down to a steady pace, while the spinal cord grows at an even rate until maturity is attained. The rapid growth of the brain after birth and in infancy was due, I inferred, to the assemblage of the nerve elements needed to equip the brain as "the organ of the mind," while the additions made during the period of slow growth . . . were concerned with what may be called the administrative function of the brain, in its role of regulating the body. . . . The bigger the "thinking" part of the brain became, the longer and later was the period of rapid growth. (1950, 163–64)

In a table depicting the relative brain sizes of monkeys, apes, and man, Keith shows how "The column representing the human brain towers above those of the Anthropoids, and they in turn rise above those of the Cercopithecidae" (1895a, 291). The rocket-like rise of the [human] nerve curves during the period of infantility I take to indicate a rapid deposition of nervous tissue which is to serve as substratum for functions required at an early stage of existence, and which entirely masks the coexisting increase due to the corporeal concomitant" (289). If the "rocket-like rise" and "towering" of the human brain correspond to the "upper storeys" of the mind, it could be through a retention of fetal rates of growth, due perhaps to a hormonal shift, that the human brain is endowed with the faculty of reason.[3] By moving faster—by extending the period of rapid fetal growth in the individual—the human brain would cross the "Cerebral Rubicon" which separates it from ape brains.[4]

According to this interpretation, Keith could have depicted the phylogenetic transformation of the human brain as a relatively rapid,

---

3. An anonymous editorial in *Nature* reviewed Keith's speech: "It may of course be said that variations in the regulative system—in hormone production in particular—stimulated brain development, and were associated with temporal variation in the relative length of the antenatal and infantile archs in the trajectory of life; and Sir Arthur evidently looks to hormone keys to open locks to which they have not yet been fitted by the evolutionist. But our suggestion is that more must be made of the psychical and social factors in man's emergence" (Anonymous 1927, 322).

4. Keith identified the lower boundary of human brain size (1000 cc.) as the "Cerebral Rubicon."

and even sudden, event: the retention of fetal rates of growth might be due to a shift in hormone level. Yet the rate of brain evolution is almost glacial, according to his 1925 phylogenetic diagram: the expansion of the brain begins in the middle Miocene and continues into the Pliocene and Pleistocene. As we recall, even the orthograde "revolution" was a gradual event, beginning in the Eocene and extending into the Oligocene. It occurred by the straggling of muscle cells "too high or too low," rather than by a sudden rearrangement.

Keith's belief in slow physiological change in turn influenced his interpretation of fossils. Of all the fossil species discovered by 1925, when Keith drew his phylogeny, only three had cranial capacities below the human standard: *Australopithecus*, *Pithecanthropus*, and the recently discovered *Sinanthropus*, or Peking man. None of these prehumans is depicted as ancestral in Keith's phylogeny. The brain of *Australopithecus* is too small for its geological age. The brain of Java man "has just reached the human threshold," but it is also too recent to be directly ancestral. Especially when compared to the enormous brain of Neanderthal man, "one is compelled to believe that the human brain had attained a greater size than that of the Java man at the end of the Pliocene period" (1911, 136); it would take "nothing short of a biological miracle to turn the brain of *Pithecanthropus* into the brain of Neanderthal Man in the short space of two or three hundred thousand years" (1917, 84). "To transform this ancient type of Java into the most primitive of living human types, evolution would have to proceed at an extremely quick pace. It is easier to believe that *Pithecanthropus* represents the persistence of an early Pliocene type than that it represents the stage reached in human evolution at the end of that period" (1925b, 320). Even the larger brained *Sinanthropus* or Peking man must be a persistent type for it appears too late—in the early Pleistocene—to be directly ancestral.

> Even if we take the highest estimates for the Pleistocene period—a duration of 1.5 million years—the changes which would convert the brain of *Sinanthropus* into that of La Chapelle man would have to be of unexpected rapidity. . . . There is, however,

another possibility. The men of Java and China may not have represented the highest stage reached in human brain development in early Pleistocene times; elsewhere in the world there might have been a higher form of humanity (1930, 940–41).

In fact, Keith finds a better ancestral candidate in his own country.

Peking man lived at the eastern end of the Old World; his contemporary—Piltdown man—lived at the Western end of it. Piltdown man, in spite of his ape-like canine teeth and his simian chin, makes an infinitely closer approach to the modern type of man than does Peking man. The latter has the flattened head which we knew of only in Java man; he has the great bony beam across his forehead which we meet with in Neanderthal man, and many other traits which give him a claim . . . to be considered as a possible ancestor of the Neanderthal races. . . . On the other hand, Piltdown has none of the Neanderthalian or Javanese traits; the conformation of his skull bones and of his head herald features of modern man. (941)

The Piltdown discovery made a deep impression on Keith. Indeed, he undertook *The Antiquity of Man* in order to account for it within his own phylogenetic framework. Keith's preoccupation is evident in the gold-tooled engraving of Piltdown on the cover of the book and in the many diagrams inside, showing other fossil skulls in comparison with the superimposed profile of Piltdown. The transforming effect of Piltdown, made graphic in these diagrams, is evident also in his description of the men of Peking and Java in the above passage (taken from a later article). Despite the small brain which earlier made him an unlikely ancestor to the La Chapelle Neanderthal man, Peking is here considered a possible Neanderthal ancestor. His flattened head and supraorbital ridges are defined as "Neanderthalian or Javanese traits" and are seen in contrast—"on the other hand"—to Piltdown, who "has none of these traits"; who is "uncontaminated" and thus "free" to become human. Though Keith did not describe Neanderthal man in explicitly pathological terms, there is a sense that his overgrown features, such as the great bony beam, are somehow responsible for his extinction, that even the large Neanderthal brain is in a sense hypertrophied and possibly abnormal in function. Though Neanderthal man "did not perish for lack of brains" (1930, 942), he may have gained his large brain not by maintaining rapid fetal rates of growth during infancy but by continuous slow growth into adulthood. If so, it might have developed to serve the needs of the corporeal concomitant, rather than the "organ of mind," as in humans. Whether or not the Neanderthals have too much brain, they undoubtedly have too much brawn. They fall on the wrong side of a symbolic dualism more basic than health versus disease: mind versus matter.

Lacking the heavily built features of the Neanderthal skull, Piltdown man appears free to become human—like the fetus, a "herald" of modern humanity. Even the anthropoid features of its jaws and teeth—"the chief obstacles to placing the Piltdown type on the direct line of our ancestry"—appear smaller in light of its large and nonrobust brain case. Keith observes that the large Piltdown palate, which he reconstructs to be gorilla-sized, appears much smaller when it is viewed in relation to the skull cap. Seen in relation to the skull, the ape-sized palate comes to look just the right size for a creature on its way to becoming human.

Keith's reconstruction of the Piltdown palate was made in the light of the Piltdown skull, yet the skull, which consisted of fragments, was itself a matter for interpretation. The controversy over the reconstruction of the Piltdown skull is as well-known as the Huxley-Owen debate; it was here that Keith and Elliot Smith began their famous rivalry. Keith's original entry into the field was directed not against Elliot Smith but against the eminent British paleontologist Arthur Smith Woodward. It was Smith Woodward who was invited by Charles Dawson, the discoverer of the remains, to present the Piltdown skull to the scientific community. Keith described the occasion in his *Autobiography*:

> Soon after [their discovery] the Piltdown fossils were shown at a crowded meeting of the Geological Society. I took part in the discussion. I pointed out that the articulation on the skull for

the lower jaw was similar to that of modern man and that an ape-like canine was incompatible with this form of joint. In this Smith Woodward proved me to be in the wrong, for in the following year (1913) the missing canine was found; it was not so big as my opponent had supposed, but it was simian in shape. So in the first round of the controversy honours went to Smith Woodward. (1950, 325).

Keith next turned his attention to Smith Woodward's reconstruction of the Piltdown braincase: "I fitted the various fragments of the skull into what I believed to be their proper places, and became convinced that Smith Woodward had deprived Piltdown of some 250 or 300 c.c. [cubic centimeters] of his brain-space" (1925a, 326). Keith more than compensated for his opponent's stinginess: his reconstruction of the skull grants Piltdown a brain size of 1,500 c.c. compared to Smith Woodward's 1,050 c.c. Elliot Smith, who entered the fray to defend Smith Woodward and also to question the views of Keith, granted Piltdown man a cranial capacity of 1,070 c.c. While this discrepancy may be traced to the profound theoretical differences between Keith and Elliot Smith concerning the overall course and mechanism of human evolution, it turned on a more technical point. Elliot Smith perceived asymmetry in the brain of Piltdown man, whereas Keith reserved this feature for later humans. In the light of the uncovering of the Piltdown hoax, we know that both men were right: the brain case of Piltdown, which belonged to a modern man, was asymmetrical *and* it was large. Ironically, Keith arrived at the best estimate about the size not because he modernized the skull but because he believed it to be more primitive—that is, more symmetrical—than modern humans.

Keith's views on Piltdown must be seen in the light of his belief in yet another misleading British find, Galley Hill man. Discovered in 1888, these remains, which were modern human in form, were found in a middle Pleistocene stratum and assigned a date of 200,000 years. Unlike most of his British colleagues, including Elliot Smith, who believed Galley Hill man to be a recent burial, Keith accepted this discovery as an authentic fossil.[5] This belief, in turn, led him to accept the antiquity of other pre-Mousterian modern humans found at Ipswich, Tilbury, and Dartford. Keith's belief in the antiquity of these modern men is reflected in his interpretation of Piltdown man: Piltdown man's brain had to be big in order to evolve into the Galley Hill type in the space of a few hundred thousand years. The question remains, why did Keith, alone, accept the Galley Hill finds as authentic? Keith first studied the remains of Galley Hill in 1909, the same year as his comparison between Neanderthal man and the acromegalic. By accepting Galley Hill, he found a more suitable ancestor for the Cro-Magnons and avoided placing the hypertrophic Neanderthals in the direct human lineage. In his 1915 phylogeny, he draws another line to carry this form—and others such as *Pithecanthropus* and *Sinanthropus*—away from the pure human line which, cleared of such unwieldy forms, is unencumbered by fossils altogether.

Even Piltdown lies on a sidebranch according to Keith's 1915 phylogenetic conception. The Piltdown skull is too massive to be called a member of our genus. "When we sum up all the characters which Dr. Smith Woodward has portrayed in this new form of being —the anthropoid characters of the mouth, teeth, and face, the massive and ill-filled skull, the simian characters of the brain and its primitive and pre-human general appearance—one feels convinced that he was absolutely justified in creating a new genus of the family Hominidae for its reception. This new genus he named *Eoanthropus*" (1915, 336). Happily for Smith Woodward and Keith, Eo-*anthropus* may still be called an English-*man*.

CIVILIZATION: in which the conflict between man and nature escalates into a (8) *greater struggle*; "Civilization thwarts Nature's Plan," but man's (9) *triumph* over the natural world brings uncertain rewards as "the ancient tribal organization employed by Nature in the evolution of human beings is brought into a state of disorder."

5. Galley Hill man is, in fact, a recent burial.

By the middle Pleistocene the anatomical transition to humanity is complete, since all fossil forms have brains well within the range of modern humans. From this point, evolutionary fates are determined less by the physiological machinery under nature's employ and more by the way these large-brained humans use reason to shape the environment. Not that physical changes cease once the Cerebral Rubicon is crossed; nor is the brain exempt from nature's laws of variation. Though the donor equips all of these middle Pleistocene forms with large brains, she does not endow them equally with reason. These differences in brain endowment are seen in man's artifacts more clearly than in his skull morphology.

Like many prehistorians of his day, Keith interprets the archeological record typologically—to measure general levels of cultural advancement rather than to reconstruct specific behaviors, and also to date the fossil record. But even the archeological record is not a clear indicator of progress. Advanced technologies could have developed over time as the product of greater experience rather than superior minds. Conversely, primitive technologies might have required enormous intellects: "We of a later generation, with a fertility of mechanical invention, can little understand the great brain which was necessary to make the first steps toward human civilization" (1911, 112). Indeed, our brains are smaller than those of some Cro-Magnon men. The growth of civilization, with its "fertility of mechanical invention," has actually inhibited human evolution: "Man's body and brain are fashioned to serve in the execution of a great scheme of progress by evolutionary means; that scheme is being foiled by civilization—man's greatest discovery" (1928, 320).

It is only later in the story that this antagonism between nature and civilization develops. To begin, civilization, especially technology, operates as part of nature's machinery. By advancing a hunting way of life, tools and weapons function to keep human groups separated. "Each tribe is confined to a sharply demarcated hunting-territory; if it passes beyond this tribal frontier, then it encroaches on the hunting-rights of neighbouring tribes and will have to fight or retreat" (315). Hunting reinforces the machinery of segregation by confining tribes to specific tracts of land; it also calls into play "a selective mechanism represented by changing environment and inter-racial competition." "In changing environment are to be reckoned gradual submergence of occupied lands, extension of desert zones, and the spread and retreat of Arctic conditions" (320). Though Keith depicts the environment as a selective force, his landscape differs significantly from Darwin's: harsh environments such as deserts and glaciers are emphasized, but more as obstacles to miscegenation than as Darwinian challenges to survival. Even his conception of interra-cial competition differs from Darwin's: according to the principle of segregation, it is better to retreat than to fight one's foes and risk upsetting tribal boundaries.

Nevertheless, man appears at his most aggressive during this long episode of Keith's narrative. He is a killer and at the same time a devoted family man—which, in part, is why he kills. "He, his wife, and children had to make a home in any natural shelter which of-fered; every morning the family set out to scrape a subsistence from such a table as the season spread before them, and in winter the table was miserably bare. Killing was their occupation; the more they killed the more they rejoiced. They had to slay savage animals in order that they might live to eat; they had to kill game in order that they might eat to live" (1925f, 35). Following his habit of kill-ing other animals, man develops the habit of killing other humans. This new occupation entails a refinement of his morals, as well as his technology. Just as stones may be used as weapons or tools—to destroy or build—laws are also divided into two sets with differing functions: "One was for use inside his tribal frontier; the other came into action when he passed beyond it. To kill a fellow-tribesman was murder; to kill the member of another tribe was heroism" (45).

By transforming tribal boundaries into a system of behavioral rules—of rights and wrongs—hunting establishes the fundamental division upon which civilization is based: good versus evil. Indeed, religion itself is founded along the lines established by these tribal boundaries. "The rules which held within the tribe became in due time the basis for the Christian code. No primitive tribe could con-tinue to exist unless the law of Christ was obeyed within it; nor could Nature's ends be served unless this law became that of Satan the moment the tribesman reached his frontier" (45). To begin, religion functioned as part of the machinery which nature employs to consolidate the tribe. And yet as Keith describes, religion and nature now work at cross-purposes. "Christ's mission in life was to break down tribal boundaries—the fences which Nature had set up with such infinite ingenuity and patience. He sought to make mankind one tribe, and the intratribal practice of mercy the common law of the world" (49–50).

Yet it is not a morally based act but a technologically based one which first turned the tide and set nature and civilization in opposition.

> When we search for the force which has destroyed the tribal organization of ancient Europe, we have to dive into the prehistory of the Middle East. Somewhere in this part of the world was made the discovery on which our modern civilization is based—the art of agriculture. The tribe or tribes who made this discovery had gained an advantage over all their hunting neighbours: their numbers must have multiplied as their food-supply increased; sooner or later their tribal territory could not contain them and they had to spread. It is in keeping with all we know to regard the Caucasoid East as the cradle of civilization, and to suppose that from this centre wave after wave spread westwards across Europe finally breaking on our islands. Tribal territories were broken down, and the ancient tribal organization employed by Nature in the evolution of human beings was brought into a state of disorder. Civilization has everywhere in the Caucasoid area queered Nature's plan of Evolution. (1928, 318)

The discovery of agriculture is a turning point, "the most critical chapter of man's long history." With waves of humanity crashing, and tribal boundaries bursting at the seams, this is the most action-packed episode in Keith's tale. It is a period of conflict and, ultimately, revolution. Unlike the orderly "structural revolution" that transformed the body of man, the "agricultural revolution" is a subversive movement: it "queers" nature's plan of evolution. Keith announces this struggle for power in newspaper-headline style: "Civilization Thwarts Nature's Plan." The contest during this last episode is not between nature and man for, however aggressive he appears, man is still a puppet pulled now by two sets of strings: nature and the new god, civilization. These two donors fight for control of man through their various machines: the machinery of evolution and the machinery of technology, respectively.

Though the opposition between nature and civilization motivates the last episode in Keith's account, it is their similarity, emphasized by Keith's use of metaphor, that makes them fit opponents. Not only are they both mechanical, they are both rational. Though the basic terms of comparison—purposeful, collective action —derive largely from the world of human affairs, it is clear that biology has the upper hand in the analogy: it is civilization that imitates the embryo rather than the reverse; it is civilization that has learned nature's rules, and to the same ends: the retention of fetal traits. "Foetal inheritance becomes more and more possible for man because civilisation tends to make man's world into a protective womb" (1928, 821).

Yet the external womb of civilization competes with the internal womb in which nature conducts her species-building experiments. Civilization, which entails the growth of industry and nations, as well as of science and art, tends to unite people rather than segregate them. Though technology grants man a fertility of mechanical invention, it inhibits the tribal machinery. Not only does it damage the machinery employed by nature in the evolution of human beings, it threatens the human body.

> Beyond a doubt civilisation is submitting the human body to a vast and critical experiment. It is not only the alimentary system which is being subjected to new conditions; the bony and muscular framework of our bodies are also being subjected to novel stresses. . . . Our forefathers when they arrived in Western Europe were hunters; their bodies were unaccustomed to either manual labour or an indoor life; under the stress of civilisation the hunter's body has to serve modern needs. . . . Civilisation has

laid bare some of the weak spots in the human body, but the conditions which have provoked them are not of Nature's ordaining but of man's choosing. (1925d, 821–22)

Man is again the subject of an experiment, conducted not by nature but by civilization. Though man may "choose" civilization, it is now beyond his rational control; it is in fact "out of control." Civilization has become the antithesis of nature's orderly and controlled experiment. Not only has it thrown nature's plan of tribal organization into disarray, it has "plunged" nature's creation, man's body, into a state of disorder. For Keith the true explanation of man's so-called vestigial structures is not that they are useless but that they are "disorders": "structural disharmon[ies] occasioned by the conditions which civilisation has entailed on us." "The evidence, such as it is, leads us to believe that when the appendix breaks down under the conditions of modern civilisation, it does so not because it is 'vestigial,' but because of its inability to withstand the conditions to which it is being exposed" (867).

According to Keith, the significance of these "structural disharmonies" is best expressed by the term "abiotrophy," or "wrong growth," which was coined by Sir William Gowers to describe "the premature senility on the part of any organ or structure." "In this sense the appendix is an abiotrophic structure, one which is apt to suffer from a disordered life-history; in a large proportion of Europeans it becomes abiotrophic or senile when other parts of the body are in full vigour" (867). And there are others—hernia, flat-feet, dental cavities, impacted wisdom teeth. All are disorders—structural disharmonies; signs of old age. And yet they are found in greatest number among Europeans who live in the most advanced and presumably most womblike civilizations.

Despite Keith's analogy, civilization and nature's womb are worlds apart. Indeed, they are antitheses. Compared to the embryo—the picture of harmony and health—civilization presents an opposite image: disorder and disease. Nor does civilized man, with his fallen arches, bear much resemblance to his nimble ancestor flying through the trees. Still, there may be a deeper connection between modern man and his forebears. Though in possession of civilization, modern man is not really civilized. "Below the surface of things . . . the beggar of paleolithic times is precisely the same man who becomes the millionaire of today. Man has changed the outward appearance of his life, but his body, and we may presume, his inward self remain much the same. Man has climbed up the ladder of civilisation, but it is the same old body and the same old brain he has dragged with him" (1925f, 36–37).

Nonetheless, Keith's hero is deeply transformed: from a "favoured and carefree child" of nature into a tormented and decrepit adult. In dragging himself up the ladder of civilization, man feels the burden of nature and thus the futility of his task. It is in this pose that Keith's human looks most like the traditional anthropogenic hero: a being made for happiness who can never reach that end because he is caught between worlds; a creature doomed to go no further because, finally, he is human.

Keith's hero, depicted as a puppet and pawn, never gains control of his own story. As we will see, fossils are vehicles for the author's themes rather than determining factors of Keith's narrative.

Of all the fossils Keith discusses, Galley Hill man best illustrates the theme of the antiquity of man. His Chellean implements demonstrate that he could "use [his] brains and his hands to carry out an art which requires a high degree of skill and design," but it is his age that earns him the title of hero. By appearing before the Neanderthal race—by sacrificing himself as a man before his time—he preserves the purity of the human line. Though he is replaced in Europe by Neanderthal man, Galley Hill's descendants triumphantly return there in the form of the Cro-Magnons.

Galley Hill further serves to draw our attention to the real protagonist of Keith's narrative: nature. By remaining separate and different from Neanderthal, Galley Hill provides fossil proof of the effectiveness of her dual machinery. Although it breaks the single sequence and is thus "disorderly," the coexistence and conflict of Galley Hill and Neanderthal is a symptom of man and nature in a state of evolutionary harmony and health. It is only because Keith has such a concept of the natural course of human evolution that he can assign Galley Hill—who plays a minor role in other early-twentieth-century accounts and today is altogether forgotten—such an important role in human evolution.

Similarly, Keith discerns order among the welter of such coexisting Upper Paleolithic fossil forms as Combe Capelle, Grimaldi, Boskop, and Cro-Magnon; for a high degree of racial differentiation is the sign of a species in good health. Of these, the Cro-Magnon race stands out as "one of the finest the world has ever seen." "When we look at [these] forerunners of our kind, the disappearance of Neanderthal man can be understood." Indeed, their appearance signifies the climax of Keith's story; after they disappear human brains and stature never again reach the Cro-Magnon standard. Though Keith attaches little importance to these measures, there is a sense that with the passing of Cro-Magnon, humanity begins its evolutionary decline.

It is at this point in the fossil record that the tide turns, and the productive struggle between men is transformed into the doomed struggle between nature and civilization. Not only do brain size and stature decrease, but there is also a decrease in racial diversity. It is not long after this that the agricultural or "Neolithic" revolution occurs. By this time human remains are hardly different from living humans:

> So far as the physical appearance of Tilbury Man [from the Neolithic of England] is concerned he might be one of us. . . . But . . . it would mean little to compare this ancient Englishman to the average Briton of to-day. We British, like every nation under the sun, are a diverse people. It seems better for the purposes of comparison to take an individual—and the one I select is the notorious Englishman of the eighteenth century, who after a life of crime was hanged, and had his skeleton handed down to posterity in the celebrated Museum of the Royal College of Surgeons, England to the great benefit of many generations of medical students. (1912, 14)

It may be assumed that Tilbury man was spared this criminal's fate and that he died an unhung hero.

From this point on, Keith draws his characters from the historical rather than the prehistorical record. Strictly speaking, this point could signify the end of Keith's story. Yet human evolution is far from over. It continues where Keith's own story began—in the world of the present. Despite Keith's preoccupation with ancient human skulls, for him the answers to the mystery of human evolution lay not in fossils but in flesh and blood; not in the dark jungles of the past but in the well-lit laboratories of the twentieth century, and also on its battlefields: "The Great War has swept over Europe, uncovering primitive traits and impulses which lie deeply buried in human nature. As a sequel to the war came the demands of small nationalities for separation and independence. . . . The small-nation movement is due to a recrudescence of the old machinery of racial evolution: in the atmosphere of war submerged human impulses came surging into activity" (1928, 318). Once again, the tide may turn, this time allowing nature to rise up and reinstate her "old machinery." War may prove nature's greatest weapon in her struggle to regain control over humanity.

Keith's story of human evolution clearly bears the mark of his times, not only in its scientific discoveries but also in its historical developments. This mark is evident in his image of the donor—the fertility goddess with her factories and machines. We might also see it in his portrait of the helpless hero—the pawn, the victim of circumstance—who, if only in passing, bears a poignant resemblance to Keith himself after the unmasking of Piltdown.

5   Elliot Smith's Tomb

G RAFTON ELLIOT SMITH died sixteen years before the
Piltdown hoax was exposed. He would have been deeply
disturbed to learn of the fraud, for though he was an
iconoclast who liked to make scientists squirm, as his
biographer A. J. E. Cave has observed, he was an ardent defender of
scientific virtue.

> While revelling in controversy, he never deliberately sought it for
> its own sake. Devastating indeed his critical pen could be, and if,
> occasionally, denunciation was over-emphatic, it was inspired not
> by personal rancor but by his Huxleian zeal for the rectification
> of error.
>
> That veritable bone of contention, the Piltdown Skull, pro-
> vided the original stimulus to Elliot Smith's prolonged occupa-
> tion with the fossil record of man's antiquity, besides affording
> opportunity for the display of his profound knowledge of cranial
> and cerebral form. (1937, 199)

Having already established his scientific reputation as the chairman
of anatomy at the University of Manchester, the forty-one-year-old
Australian was invited by Arthur Smith Woodward to make a study

of the cranial cast of the Piltdown skull. Though Elliot Smith disagreed with aspects of Smith Woodward's reproduction of the skull, he reserved his real criticism for Keith's reconstruction, and undertook his own—his first fossil replica—as a contribution to that polemic. It was Arthur Keith who drew Elliot Smith into the debate on fossil man, just as Owen drew in Huxley.

Though Elliot Smith's professional involvement with fossils was shorter lived than Keith's, his interest in the general subject of human evolution began around the same time and in much the same manner. After graduating from medical school at the University of Sydney in 1895, he was appointed demonstrator in anatomy and undertook independent research in comparative neuroanatomy. Like Keith's dissections in the jungles of Siam, Elliot Smith's early research was fruitful.

> In the congenial environment of Professor J. T. Wilson's laboratory, his early interest [in neuroanatomy] rooted and flourished, bearing as fruit a series of revolutionary, but now classic, memoirs upon the morphology of the lower mammalian brain, which brought him, whilst not yet twenty-five, international recognition and reputation. With characteristic fearlessness, yet without specialized training, Elliot Smith confidently entered a difficult field, one already tilled by many great anatomists—Owen, Broca, Edinger, Retzius, Ziehen and Zuckerkandl on the continent. (188)

Inspired by the great mystery of the cerebral cortex, the dominant structure of the human brain, Elliot Smith began his iconoclastic career by studying the lowliest of human cerebral structures: the rhinencephalon or smell-brain. He demonstrated that, as the smell-brain decreases, the cerebral cortex increases in the more "progressive" mammals, a trend which reaches its culmination in humans.

Having demonstrated the relationship between the highest and lowest parts of the brain, Elliot Smith next turned his attention to the connections between the right and left cerebral hemispheres. Most neuroanatomists believed that the brains of all mammals had a corpus callosum, or connecting fiber-band; Elliot Smith showed that only the placental mammals (in contrast to the marsupials and monotremes) have such a structure and that consequently only they possess a true associative cortex or "neopallium" (a term which he invented). According to Elliot Smith, the neopallium was the essential factor in bringing the higher mammals, and thus humans, into being. We shall see that the rise of the neopallium and the diminution of the smell-brain is the starting point for Elliot Smith's narrative.

Elliot Smith moved to postdoctoral work at Cambridge University in 1896; two years later, he accepted the chair of anatomy at the University of Cairo. There he was drawn into a study of Egyptian pyramids and rock-cut tombs. His student Frederic Wood Jones later recalled his unconventional demeanor in the field. "His geniality, his composure and his apparent idleness were so out of keeping with the generally accepted picture that it was difficult to realize that the schoolboy companion of the Tawaf was the genius who had caused so much of the structure of the brain to be clear to all men" (1938, 148). Elliot Smith's further observations on the spread of culture in the Nile Valley would come to fruition many years later in his diffusionist theory of the origin of civilization, which provides the basis for a later episode of his narrative of human evolution. The protagonist of that episode—man on his way to civilization—appears much like Elliot Smith himself: a genius in Egypt.

But his main interest during this time continued to be cerebral structure and function. In a series of publications beginning in 1901, he explored the evolutionary implications of his comparison of mammalian cerebral structures. The image of Elliot Smith as a young maverick, crossing disciplinary boundaries, is evident in his own writings on the subject. In an article published in 1903, "On the morphology of the brain in the Mammalia," Elliot Smith demurely tackles the "vexed" question of the taxonomic relationship of the lemurs and the apes: "It would, indeed, be presumptuous to attempt such a difficult task, which has baffled many zoologists with the best equipment for performing it. All that I am concerned with at present is the setting forth of such evidence as the brain affords, and the determination of its value as an index of the affinity of its possessor to other mammals" (417).

He concludes by attacking the traditional view of zoologists that the lemurs should be classified apart from the apes. After pointing out the cerebral homologies of the two groups, he offers a "working hypothesis" for an equally challenging problem: the ancestry of the lemurs.

> The brain of the Primates was derived from some Insectivore-like type, the cerebral hemispheres of which attained a precocious development and, as one of the expressions of their greatness, bulged backward over the cerebellum. In consequence of this great extension of the "physical organ of the associative memory of visual, auditory, and tactile sensations," the sense of smell lost the predominance which it exercised in the primitive mammal (and in all the Orders of recent mammals), and the olfactory parts of the brain rapidly dwindled. (422)

Inserted "merely as a slender bond connecting certain facts," this hypothesis forges a central link: between the rise of the neopallium and the fall of the olfactory sense. This link provides the main theme for his famous 1912 British Association address, "The evolution of man," and his classic 1924 book of the same title.

Elliot Smith's classic *The Evolution of Man* was intended, like Huxley's *Man's Place in Nature*, to provide basic instruction in the subject of human evolution. Elliot Smith conceived of his book, not as a guidebook to recent fossil discoveries, like Keith's *Antiquity of Man*, but as a textbook, giving guidance in the "general principles" of human evolution.

> At the present there is no book that explains these general principles in the only logical way they are susceptible of interpretation, namely as an historical inquiry into the circumstances of Man's origin and descent. It is essential that the student should aim at understanding Man's pedigree: for until some clear conception of the sequence of changes through which the ancestors of the Human Family passed in their progress toward the attainment of Man's estate it is useless to understand how the distinctively human powers of intelligence emerged (1924, v).

Accordingly, Elliot Smith presents two pedigrees in the foreword of his book: one showing the relationships of the different families of the Order Primates and another the relationships of the different genera, species, and races of the Human Family. This arrangement is in one sense misleading, for though they appear first in the book, these two genealogies were added last; they are the only new contributions to the book, which otherwise consists of three previously published essays, including "The evolution of man," published more than ten years earlier.[1] Elliot Smith began to consider the sequence of changes and the essential condition of progress long before he drew these genealogies. Methodologically, his pedigrees represent his conclusions rather than his starting point.

Elliot Smith himself, however, insists that his expository sequence —phylogenies first—is also the sound investigative sequence.

> In the days when only a very few fragments of bone and chipped flint provided all the information available for the study of Primitive Man, a scaffolding of hypothesis was necessary in order to make any sort of edifice of such broken and scanty debris. But now that so much more material is available it is possible to build up a structure capable of standing by itself. Hence this scaffolding is not only no longer necessary, but it interferes with the view of the building. (55)

Elliot Smith presents his pedigree as a free-standing monument, and yet like Keith's phylogenetic tree, it is a scaffolding of hypothesis connecting together very few fossils. The direct line of human descent is fossil-free except for Piltdown, and even this fossil form does not occupy a definite position. Elliot Smith's neuroanatomical perspective may be represented more clearly than the fossil record in his pedigree: phylogenetic branches resemble nerve processes running off a central spine (Keith's phylogenies, in contrast, look like anastomosing arterial systems). Whether or not Elliot Smith drew

1.   Chapter 1 of *The Evolution of Man* is a reissue of Elliot Smith's 1912 address, "The Evolution of Man," the second and third chapters are reprints of a 1916 address to the British Academy, entitled "Primitive Man," and a discourse delivered in 1924, "The Human Brain," respectively.

his genealogies with a map of the central nervous system in mind, in depicting the line of human descent as a well-defined central course he expresses a general principle which he had arrived at through his earlier neuroanatomical studies: "If all the factors in his emergence are not yet known, there is one unquestionable, tangible factor that we can seize hold of and examine—the steady and uniform development of the brain along a well-defined course throughout the Primates right up to Man—which must give us the fundamental reason for 'man's emergence and ascent,' whatever other factors may contribute toward that consummation" (20).

The real purpose of *The Evolution of Man* is to resurrect this general principle.

> The study of the brain and mind [should be] the first care of the investigator of human origins. Charles Darwin, with his usual perspicuity, fully realized this; but since his time the role of intelligence and its instruments has been almost wholly ignored in these discussions, or, when invoked at all, wholly irrelevant aspects of the problem have usually been considered. There can be no doubt that this neglect of the evidence revealed in the comparative anatomy of the brain is in large measure due to the discredit cast upon this branch of knowledge by the singularly futile pretensions of some of the foremost anatomists who opposed Darwin's views. (22)

Elliot Smith's aim is to rehabilitate the view, thrown into disrepute by the Owen-Huxley debate, that the brain is the primary factor in human evolution. He confronts the alternative view, held by Keith among others, that bipedalism led the way in human evolution.

> If the erect posture is to explain all, why did not the Gibbon become a man in Miocene times or earlier? The whole of my argument has aimed at demonstrating that it is the steady growth and specialization of the brain that has been the fundamental factor in leading Man's ancestors step by step upward from the lowly Insectivore status, and through every earlier phase (Amphibian and Reptilian) in the evolution of Mammals—for Man's

brain represents the consummation of precisely those factors that throughout the Vertebrata have brought their possessors to the crest of the wave of progress. (36)

It was not the adoption of the erect attitude that made Man from an Ape, but the gradual perfecting of the brain and the slow upbringing of the mental structure, of which erectness of carriage is one of the incidental manifestations. (39)

Elliot Smith does not name Keith; nor does he identify him in his discussion of Piltdown, though he contradicts there, almost point for point, Keith's reconstruction. Keith remains unnamed, as Owen did in Huxley's book, and yet it is clear that Elliot Smith emphasizes the smallness of the Piltdown skull in opposition to Keith's larger reconstruction. The differences between him and Keith are clearly outlined in his diagrams of the Piltdown skull. Though asymmetrical, its greatest width appears at the base rather than, as Keith depicted, in the parietal region. Compared to the squarish structure shown in *The Antiquity of Man*, Elliot Smith's Piltdown skull, with its steeply sloping walls, is a pyramidal vaultlike structure.

But it is at the level of explanatory principles that Elliot Smith's polemic against Keith goes deepest. He dismisses Keith's views on hormones as "gay theories," which are "unsubstantiated by any control of experiment or observation." "While endocrine activity may influence the structure and metabolism of an individual and control his desires and behaviour, there is, as yet, not a scrap of evidence to prove that it plays the part of the determining factor in evolution" (1925, 856). Yet Elliot Smith's own views on the role of the brain are hardly better grounded. Though "the steady and uniform development of the brain" may be observed by comparing the brain of man to primates lower in the taxonomic hierarchy, there is no evidence that it is the determining factor in man's evolution. The expansion of the brain does not necessarily explain its further growth; it is not, in this regard, a sufficient cause or explanation. By his own admission, the evidence for this factor is circumstantial. Elliot Smith proposes his general principles "in the only logical way they are susceptible of interpretation, namely as an historical inquiry into the circumstances of Man's origin and descent." He presents them in the form of a narrative.[2]

For Elliot Smith, as much as for Keith, the story of human evolution will be told from within. The critical events and "struggles" go on inside the hero, in the skull-vault or brain-chamber. Elliot Smith's narrative opens with "The Struggle for Dominance between Smell and Vision." From this point, progress is measured primarily by the extent to which the power of vision extends its dominion in the brain, and only secondarily by man's success in the Darwinian struggle for existence. Once decisively annexed by vision, the brain becomes the agent of the "high power" entombed in man's cerebrum: "The human brain is the instrument of the high powers of intelligence that distinguish Man from all other living creatures. The secret of Man's most distinctive attribute is hidden in the texture of his brain, and perhaps will never be fully revealed" (1924, 135). Elliot Smith's donor lies buried in the hidden recesses of the brain, just as the creative force of Keith's account resides within the embryo. However, the power of vision does not exempt the hero from being acted upon by natural selection; in fact it provides broader exposure:

> It has been demonstrated quite definitely that Man, in virtue of these very heightened powers, which, to some observers, seem to have secured him an immunity from what Sir Ray Lankester calls 'nature's inexorable discipline of death', is constantly exposing himself to new conditions that favour the operations of natural selection, as well as other forms of 'selection' to which his increased powers of intelligent choice and his subjection to the influences of fashion and tradition expose him. (19–20)

Yet, as we will see, selective pressures are not presented until they are sought; that is, when the hero is equipped by his donor to meet them. Nor do these challenges seem to pose great threats: com-

---

2. As Peter Bowler observes, in Elliot Smith's theory, "the trend itself . . . creates a framework within which a narrative may be constructed" (1986, 13).

petition between groups plays little part in Elliot Smith's account; nor is the environment especially dangerous. "The laboratory in which, for untold ages, Nature was making her great experiments to achieve the transmutation of the base substance of some brutal Ape into the divine form of Man" (77–78) seems more like the congenial environment of Elliot Smith's medical school days than the ruthless hecatomb—the great sacrifice—of Darwin. It operates primarily by eliciting the superior mental powers within man's brain and only secondarily by eliminating the inferior individuals within a species. As we will see, the conditions of modern civilization impose greater hardship and strife than the natural environment, as in Keith's narrative.

The power of vision exposes the hero to challenges which cultivate his mind; at the same time it protects his body from the specializing influence of natural selection. According to Elliot Smith, man's progress has depended as much on keeping his body in a relatively simple or unspecialized state as on developing his cerebral cortex. This "Law of the Unspecialized" is a central tenet in Elliot Smith's narrative. It affects the ordering of fossils and events in Elliot Smith's tale, much as Bolk's Law did in Keith's story. Like that principle, the Law of the Unspecialized conveys a basic message: human evolution has been in the direction of mind rather than body.

ENCEPHALIZATION: in which (1) *the scene is set* in "the slow-moving world of the Dawn of the Age of Mammals"; (2) *the hero is introduced*, a humble but large-brained Therapsid, set apart from the rest of the animal world by its "new-found power of adaptation."

And so Elliot Smith's tale begins with "the first glimmerings of human characteristics" in the newly acquired neopallium of a primitive Therapsid, or "mammal-like reptile."

> The possession of this higher type of brain enormously widened the scope for the conscious and intelligent adaptation of the animal to varying surroundings. In the exercise of this newly acquired power of discrimination and ability to learn from indi-

vidual experience, and so appreciate the possibilities of fresh sources of food supply and new modes of life, the way was opened for an infinite series of adaptations to varying environments, entailing the structural modifications in which the enhanced plasticity of the new type of animal found expression. (27)

The primitive Therapsid is transformed into the first mammal by exercising its new mental gifts. But it is not until the corpus callosum appears that this primitive mammal is transformed into a eutherian or placental mammal.

The new breed of intelligent creatures rapidly spread throughout the whole world and exploited every mode of livelihood. The power of adaptation to the particular kind of life each group chose to pursue soon came to be expressed in a bewildering variety of specializations in structure, some for living on the earth or burrowing in it, others for living in trees or even for flight; others, again, for an aquatic existence. Some mammals became fleet of foot and developed limbs specially adapted to enhance their powers of rapid movement. They attained an early preeminence and were able to grow to large dimensions in the slow-moving world of the dawn of the Age of Mammals. Others developed limbs specially adapted for swift attack and habits of stealth successfully to prey upon their defenceless relatives. (27–28)

The world of the placental mammals is an abundant place, a land of seemingly unlimited opportunity and little conflict. The greatest danger in this Garden of Eden comes not from predators but from a more subtle source: the temptation to specialize. "Most of these groups attained the immediate success that often follows upon early specialization, but they also paid the inevitable penalty. They became definitely committed to one particular kind of life, and in so doing they sacrificed their primitive simplicity and plasticity of structure, and in great measure also their adaptability to new conditions" (28). Specialization entails a "commitment" and a "sacrifice." It also involves a "succumbing" and thus represents the fallen path, whereas the retention of primitive traits signifies the virtuous one.

> It is important to keep . . . in mind that the retention of primitive characters is often to be looked upon as a token that their possessor has not been compelled to turn aside from the straight path and adopt protective specializations, but has been able to preserve some of the plasticity associated with his primitiveness, precisely because he has not succumbed or fallen away in the struggle for supremacy. It is the wider triumph of the individual who specializes late after benefitting from the many-sided experience of early life, over him who in youth becomes tied to one narrow calling. (34–35)

The "wider triumph" is achieved by maintaining the purity and pluripotentiality of youth, as in Keith's tale. Whereas for Keith this occurs by the "blossoming" of fetal traits, including the large brain, according to Elliot Smith, the hero's burgeoning brain protects the body and therefore keeps it in its primitive mammalian condition.[3] It is only because of the protection afforded by his brain that the hero could be so physically weak. Indeed, as we will see, he is smaller and more defenseless than Darwin's ancestor. The brain does not merely compensate for his lack of tooth and claw, as in *The Descent of Man*; it actively keeps the hero from developing these specializations.

Compared to the fallen path taken by those who seek immediate success, "the highway to man's estate" looks like a country lane at this early point in Elliot Smith's narrative. Its first travellers are so lacking in physical presence that they might almost go unnoticed.

> The stock from which Man eventually emerged played a very humble role for long ages after many other Mammalian Orders had waxed great and strong. But the race is not always to the swift. The lowly group of mammals that took advantage of its insignificance to develop its powers evenly and very gradually without sacrificing in narrow specialization any of its possibili-

---

3. Elliot Smith, in explicit contrast to Keith, describes fetalization (Bolk's Law) as a kind of "inertia."

ties of future achievement, eventually gave birth to the most dominant and most intelligent of all living creatures. (28)

The race is not to the swift. As we shall see, the weak inherit the earth, as they do in Darwin's tale, gradually.

Though Elliot Smith's story begins with a primitive mammal while Darwin's begins with an ape, the hero in both cases is a small creature, slightly more intelligent than its fellows. Elliot Smith uses a living form, the tree shrew, rather than a fossil to play the role of the hero at this stage of his adventure. Of "lively disposition and great agility," this creature is still not a Primate. Only by forsaking its terrestrial home does it give rise to a new order of mammals.

ARBOREALITY: (3) *the situation changes* with the move into the trees; but it is the transfer of power from the olfactory to the visual sense which signifies "the birth of the Primates and the definite branching off from the other mammals of the line of Man's ancestry."

The move from the ground up into the trees — which occurs before the stories of Darwin and Keith even begin — is a pivotal point in Elliot Smith's narrative. Once it has occurred the story moves almost inevitably to its conclusion. The arboreal realm is the precondition for the basic dialectic of Elliot Smith's tale: the decline of the olfactory sense and the rise of vision.

With the shift into the trees vision gains a real foothold in the brain. Up to that time, it is still subordinate to olfaction.

This was due not only to the fact that the sense of smell had already installed its instruments in and taken possession, so to speak, of the cerebral hemisphere long before the advent in this dominant part of the brain of any adequate representation of the other senses, but also, and chiefly, because to a small land-grubbing animal the guidance of smell impressions, whether in the search for food or as a means of recognition of friends or enemies, sexual mates or rivals, was much more serviceable than all the other senses. Thus the small creature's mental life was lived essentially in an atmosphere of odours; and every object in the outside world was judged primarily and predominantly by smell. The senses of touch, vision, and hearing were merely auxiliary to the compelling influence of smell. (29–30)

Life in the trees poses new challenges for the once land-grubbing animal. These new environmental demands work by *summoning* mental powers within the brain rather than by *selecting* for individuals who already have them. Unable to meet the new arboreal demands for agility and speed, smell "calls to its help the senses of vision and touch and what may be called the labyrinth sense" (1927b, 13). In consequence, a "more equable balance" is brought about: large portions of the brain are "given up" to these other senses, especially to vision.

Though more equable, this redistribution leads to a neuroanatomical coup d'etat: vision "usurps" the power of olfaction. This idea, which first appeared in Elliot Smith's "working-hypothesis" of 1903, is developed in his 1912 essay. There Elliot Smith describes how "vision entirely usurped the controlling place once occupied by smell" and also discusses the consequences of this revolutionary act on the rest of the neopallium: "the whole of the neopallium felt the influence of the changed conditions. The sense of touch also shared in the effects, for tactile impressions and the related kinaesthetic sensibility, the importance of which to an agile tree-living animal is obvious, assist vision in the conscious appreciation of the nature and the various properties of the things seen, and in learning to perform agile actions which are guided by vision" (1924, 32). Vision aids the hero by enhancing his muscular skill. This ability to perform agile actions, in turn, acts as a stimulus for the neopallium.

Such habits not only tended to develop the motor cortex itself, trained the tactile and kinaesthetic senses, and linked up their cortical areas in bonds of more intimate association with the visual cortex, but they stimulated the process of specialization within or alongside the motor cortex of a mechanism for regulating the action of that cortex itself. Thus arose an organ of attention which co-ordinated the activities of the whole neopallium so as the more efficiently to regulate the various centres controlling the muscles of the body. (32)

Vision usurps cortical areas but it is a constructive force: ultimately, it gives birth to a new structure, an "organ of attention." The growth of this new prefrontal area of the brain in turn provides space for the crossing of the optic tracts and, in this way, prepares the way for stereoscopic vision. "Thus the fuller cultivation of the results of the visual powers provides a new stimulus and new means for enhancing vision itself" (146). Donors typically help the hero in pursuit of some larger interest of their own. Vision, though self-seeking, does benefit the hero, for it is by virtue of the possession of stereoscopic vision that the hero is transformed from a prosimian into a monkey in the next episode.

For the first time in Elliot Smith's tale, the role of the protagonist is assigned to a fossil—*Anaptomorphus*, an Eocene prosimian. Known only from fragments, this fossil genus is modeled closely after a living species, the Spectral Tarsier of Borneo. Elliot Smith's belief in the tarsioid ancestry of man, which is the recognized hallmark of his theory of human evolution, is graphically represented in the drawing of a tarsier on the frontispiece of his book. Though he bases his belief primarily on the supposedly apelike features of the tarsier brain (its generalized corpus callosum and features of its olfactory region and cerebral hemispheres), he also takes into account the mythology of the "curious" Spectral Tarsier, "which still haunts the forests of Borneo, Java and the neighbouring islands, and awakens in the minds of the peoples of those lands a superstitious dread—a sort of instinctive horror at the sight of the ghostlike representative of their remote Primate ancestor!" (24). Elliot Smith invokes superstition, as well as scientific fact, much as Huxley did in the opening pages of *Man's Place in Nature*. Indeed, Elliot Smith's ghostlike image is a kind of paleoanthropological descendant of the centaurs and satyrs of the "half-waking" dreams of Huxley.

BIPEDALISM: in which (4) *the hero departs* from the monkeys by the development of the erect attitude.

Despite the radical transformation which the development of the power of vision entails, the hero is, like all primates, still a modest figure.

> The primates at first were a small and humble folk, who led a quiet life, unobtrusive and safe in the branches of trees, taking small part in the competition for size and supremacy that was being waged upon the earth beneath them by their carnivorous, ungulate and other brethren. But all the time they were cultivating the equable development of all their senses and limbs, and the special development of the more intellectually useful faculties of the mind that, in the long run, were to make them the progenitors of the dominant Mammal—the Mammal destined to obtain supremacy over all others, while still retaining much of the primitive structure of limb that his competitors had sacrificed. (34)

Only in those animals whose limbs have not been corrupted by "precocious specialization" can vision cultivate muscular skill, its most important agent. The importance of muscular skill is even more critical in this episode than before. It is by means of this skill that the hero is further set apart from other primates.

> The attainment of muscular skill (and with it the enhanced ability to learn by experience) is one of the fundamental purposes of the highly developed type of brain. Man differs from all other living creatures in the range of his aptitude for education, and for learning to perform skilled movements of infinite variety and complexity. His understanding of the nature of things and the nature of the forces operating around him is largely acquired by experiment; and during the process of experimentation, understanding of the meaning of things is acquired. Hence it is perhaps no exaggeration to say that high intelligence is largely one of the results of the attainment of muscular skill. (1927b, 16)

Elliot Smith emphasizes this point in a boldface subheading: "Muscular Skill Begets Intelligence."

Vision, of course, confers muscular skill in the first place. Vision brought about the power of stereoscopy, and the monkey-stage of evolution, by operating on the muscles of the eye; the donor effects its next phylogenetic transformation to the ape stage of evolution by gaining control of the hand to perform "skilled movements."

The freeing of the hand is a central motif for Elliot Smith, as it was for his nineteenth-century predecessors.

> About a century ago, it was a popular occupation among anatomists and physiologists to write treatises upon the beautiful mechanism of the human hand, and assume that the hand had been so specialized as to become the most superb illustration of design in nature. The human hand, as a matter of fact, is an extremely primitive mechanism. It retains the same structure as the hand of the earliest mammals, and reveals a great many features that are found in the most primitive reptiles and amphibians. (1924, 36)

Nevertheless, Elliot Smith adopts the nineteenth-century view that "the hand supplies all instruments, and by its correspondence with the intellect gives him universal dominion."

> When the brain had developed in such a way as to acquire greatly heightened powers of initiating and directing skilled movements of increasing degrees of complexity and refinement, it was able to use this unspecialized member for an endless variety of new purposes. This manual instrument, being still free from specialization, was plastic, and could be adapted to almost any purpose the brain directed. The human limbs that have become specialized are the legs. The legs are highly modified in adaptation to a new mode of progression that is distinctive of Man. It was the transformation of the feet that played a large part in liberating the hands from the work of locomotion. (36)

The erect posture is achieved by liberating the already unspecialized hand to perform "an endless variety of new purposes," and not as in

Haeckel's account, by the forelimbs becoming more specialized: by "more exclusively adopting and retaining the function of grasping and handling." Elliot Smith's conception of the liberation of the unspecialized hand differs also from that of Darwin. In the *Descent of Man*, the delicate use of the hands depends in the first instance on enhancing the sense of touch and secondarily on developing the mind, whereas in Elliot Smith's account the order is the opposite.

> The development of hands capable of performing skilled manipulations, out of which emerges . . . higher knowledge and intelligence, and the erect attitude, which by freeing the hands from the function of locomotion enables them to be devoted entirely to skilled movement and tactile discrimination are not the *primary* cause of man's high state of intelligence. They are merely the means used by the brain to achieve these great results. The erect attitude is rather one of the expressions of the enhancement of muscular skill: but in turn it becomes a means of still further adding to this skill by freeing the hands and enabling man to adopt the erect posture. When this happens he is able the better to use his powers of vision, and to bring his body into a position adapted for the display of skill. (1927b, 16)

Yet it is unclear what kinds of coordinated actions are displayed by the newly erect hero. Considering the sharp line between experimentation and invention that Elliot Smith later draws, it is probable that the hands are used, at first, to explore and manipulate branches and twigs rather than to manufacture tools and weapons.[4] The role assigned to the hindlimbs is more problematic. Though the feet "played a large part in liberating the hands," Elliot Smith barely discusses the leg. Nor does he describe man's "distinctive mode of progression."

---

4. Elliot Smith speculated in his 1912 essay: "Once the Simian ancestor of Man began to anticipate the consequences of his acts and put this knowledge and the growing appreciation of the powers of his hands to useful purpose, for using weapons, or even making them, the erect attitude would become a regular habit, so as to emancipate his hands entirely for their new duties" (1912, 594). For some reason, this passage is omitted from his 1924 version.

I do not propose to discuss the progressive changes that were gradually effected in the legs and feet to make them adequate to maintain the body in the erect attitude. The admirable series of memoirs by Dr. Dudley J. Morton has demonstrated how conclusive a proof the structure of the foot affords of Man's kinship to the Gorilla and of the fact that the series of changes that have been so gradually transforming the foot in the Primates was not completed when the Human Family emerged, but was continued in its extinct members until the type of foot distinctive of *Homo sapiens* emerged. (158)

Elliot Smith's use of Morton as a reference is in one respect, curious. Though Morton demonstrated the similarities between the feet of gorillas and humans, he nonetheless believed man's arboreal ancestors to have been gibbonlike forms whose hooklike hands were specialized for progressing from tree to tree, whereas Elliot Smith's hero requires unspecialized hands adapted for a variety of skilled manipulations.

As related in the passage above, Morton's description takes Darwin's gradualism to such an extreme degree that it gives the impression that the differentiation of the feet—"completed" and, by implication, "fully adaptive," only in very recent times—must have been exempt from the law of natural selection. Given that the demand for agility and quickness of movement stimulated the growth of the visual sense, locomotory skill should itself have been a primary adaptive requirement in Elliot Smith's account. Considering, too, the role played by the "wanderings" of the hero in the next episode of his tale, his perfunctory treatment of bipedalism is surprising. On the other hand, it is consistent with his main argument: the upright posture is subordinate and contingent to the developing brain, and in particular to the power of vision.

The upright posture is also the means by which the eyes, raised now to a new vantage point, come to oversee the body:

in Monkeys (and certain other mammals in which vision plays an important part in guiding movements) the eyes begin to assume the function of regulating posture and muscle-tone. . . .

The increasing influence of vision as the guiding sense added to the significance of the cortex as a posture-regulating instrument. This was an important factor in the development of the erect attitude in Man, which is maintained by conscious activity and is not an automatic posture to the same extent as that of four-footed animals is. (1927, 161)

Whereas Keith located the postural maintenance mechanism in the limbs, Elliot Smith locates it in the neopallium. So dominating is the power of the brain that in contrast to Keith's portrait, with its pleurae, muscles and bones, Elliot Smith's hero hardly seems to have a body. This impression is reinforced in the following passage. "The erect attitude, infinitely more ancient than man himself, is not the real cause of Man's emergence from the simian stage; but it is one of the factors made use of by the expanding brain as a prop still further to extend its growing dominion, and by fixing and establishing in a more decided way this erectness it liberated the hand to become the chief instrument of Man's further progress" (1924, 41). Elliot Smith conveys here his thematic priorities. In the image of the body as a "prop" for an expanding brain we see most vividly how he places mind over body.

The upright posture lags much further behind the brain than in Keith's account, but its origin is traced here to the same period. "In the remote Oligocene, a Catarrhine ape, nearly akin to the ancestors of the Indian sacred monkey *Semnopithecus*, became definitely specialized in structure in adaptation for the assumption of the erect attitude. This type of early anthropoid has persisted with relatively slight modifications in the Gibbon of the present day" (1924, 37). Though this extinct gibbonlike form (presumably *Propliopithecus* from the Fayum of Egypt) comes close to filling the role of the hero at this early upright stage, he falls short: "But if the earliest Gibbons were already able to walk upright, how is it, one might ask, that they did not begin to use their hands, thus freed from the work of progression on the earth, for skilled work, and at once become men? The obvious reason is that the brain had not yet attained a sufficiently high stage of development to provide skilled work, apart from the tree climbing, of biological usefulness for these competent hands to do" (37). Elliot Smith asks why this creature did not begin to use its hands, "freed from the work of progression," and yet as was earlier pointed out, the gibbon's hands are highly specialized for the purposes of arboreal locomotion. Elliot Smith's "obvious" answer—that the brain is not sufficiently developed to employ these "competent" hands—is also confusing, for presumably it was the brain that made the hand competent in the first place.

Elliot Smith is more cogent when discussing the brains of fossil species. Though *Pithecanthropus* and *Eoanthropus* are too recent to fill the role of hero at this early stage, their skulls attest to the gradual attainment of muscular skill and the upright posture.

> The defective development of the prefrontal and parietal areas that is so obtrusive in the Rhodesian cast is even more pronounced in *Eoanthropus*, and still more so in *Pithecanthropus*. . . . In the light of the foregoing discussion of the neopallial control of muscle-tone and its relation to the development of skill and the erect posture the deficiencies of these significant areas and their progressive expansion in the Human Family are interesting because they seem to give tangible expression to the theoretical inferences as to the gradual attainment of skill. (75)

The skulls of the Neanderthals are similarly deficient, leading Elliot Smith to another theoretical inference. "The large brain is singularly defective in the region of the forehead, and one is bound to draw the inference that Neanderthal man's hand and brain were incapable of performing those delicately skilled movements that are a distinctive prerogative of *Homo sapiens*, and the chief means whereby the latter has learned by experiment to interpret and understand the world around him" (1928b, 114). Though Neanderthal and *Homo sapiens* belong to a much later evolutionary stage, Elliot Smith's discussion of these forms illustrates a general point about the origins of the upright posture: muscular skill is man's "prerogative" in the full sense of the word, for it is both a distinctly superior advantage in his struggle to survive and a prior and exclusive right, granted specially to man by his donor.

TERRESTRIALITY: in which the hero leaves the trees and is (5) *tested* in "the hard school of experience." It is by means of the continuing help of (6) *the donor*, the power in his brain, that (7) *the hero is transformed* from an ape into a human.

Skilled in the basic arts of life, and schooled in the stimulating, if relatively safe environment of twigs and branches, the hero is now ready to descend to the ground and enter the "hard school of experience." In fact, the split between human and ape occurs even before entry to this terrestrial school, for only the most promising students are admitted.

> In one group the distinctively Primate process of growth and specialization of the brain, which had been going on in their ancestors for many thousands, even millions of years, reached a stage where the more venturesome members of the group —stimulated perhaps by some local failure of the customary food, or led forth by a curiosity bred of their growing realization of the possibilities of the unknown world beyond the trees, which had hitherto been their home—were impelled to issue forth from their forests, and seek new sources of food and new surroundings on hill and plain. The other group, perhaps because they happened to be more favourably situated or attuned to their surroundings, living in a land of plenty, which encouraged indolence in habit and stagnation of efforts and growth, were free from this glorious unrest, and remained apes. (1924, 40)

Ironically, those who are most likely to fall behind in the evolutionary journey are those who are best adapted or "attuned" to their surroundings. Whereas the apes—resting on their laurels in the trees —are "free" to remain the same, the hero, who is burdened by a "glorious unrest," is forced to leave the trees and become human.

Once reached, the terrestrial realm is a challenging but relatively unthreatening place: a backdrop for the wanderings of the hero.

By means of the land connexions during Tertiary times . . . Man's ancestors were able to wander from continent to continent until they completed the circuit of the globe; at each stage in the migrations of menotyphlous, prosimian, platyrrhine, catarrhine, and anthropoid forerunners, the unprogressive members remained in the neighbourhood of the home of their immediate ancestors, whereas those which wandered into new surroundings had to struggle for their footing, and by this striving attained a higher rank. . . .

From time to time many individuals, finding themselves amidst surroundings which were thoroughly congenial and called for no effort lagged behind; and in *Tarsius* and the Lemurs, the New World Monkeys, the Old World Monkeys, and the Anthropoid Apes we find preserved a series of these laggards, which turned aside from the highway which led to Man's estate. (33–34)

The hero at this stage of his adventure is merely following his progressive impulse. The fact that the descent to the ground, a "going down," is now the "highway," whereas life in the trees above is the "fallen" path, underscores the teleological, almost gravitational, pull that "man's estate" exerts on Elliot Smith's narrative.

Though man's apelike ancestor must now "struggle for footing and by this striving [attain] a higher rank," Elliot Smith does not choose to specify with whom or what man's apelike ancestors contend or come into conflict. Unprogressive members of the species pose no threat, because they are left behind. Competition between tribes is barely mentioned. As we have seen, the selection process occurs between members of different families or suborders—monkey versus prosimian, human versus ape—rather than between members of the same species. Nor do predators pose a great threat, for man's ancestors emerge from the trees well defended.

The realization of his abilities to defend himself upon the ground, once he had learned the use of sticks and stones as implements, would naturally have led the intelligent Ape to forsake the narrow life of the forest and roam at large in search of more abundant and attractive food and varieties of scene. . . . Thus we have come to realize the steps by which a growing brain makes it possible and desirable for the most intelligent of Apes to foresake the purely arboreal life and seek a wider sphere of activity upon the earth: they emerged from their original forest home, and in troops invaded the open country, led no doubt by the search for a more plentiful supply or a more appetizing variety of food. (1912, 595)

The social ties of these troops are very briefly described in his 1912 essay, "The evolution of man." "Like most creatures who live in the open, the adoption of social habits is one of the surest means of protection; for the eyes and ears of each individual thus become the servants of the whole community, giving warning of danger, and thus adding to the safety of the herd" (595). This passage and the previous one are omitted from *The Evolution of Man.* Perhaps Elliot Smith had grown uneasy with the issue of sociality. From the point of view of the story told here, it is perhaps best left out: to put the eyes in the role of "servants" is to undermine the ruling position occupied by vision in his narrative.

Once on the ground, the hero appears to be motivated by his donor rather than by the exigencies of his new environment: to satisfy his restless mind even more than his restless stomach. Just as man's arboreal migrations have been accompanied by "a steady development of the brain," so, too, the descent to the ground coincides with the "expansion and differentiation" of the neopallium. Indeed, the conversion from ape to man is achieved by an expansion of the territories of the brain, first, and secondarily, by man's expansion into new geographical areas.

> If one analyzes the nature of the changes which the brain has undergone in its passages from the stage represented in the Chimpanzee and Gorilla to the most primitive human condition, the outstanding factor will be found to be primarily a great expansion of the region of the cerebral cortex that is interposed between the areas into which impulses from the visual, auditory, and tactile organs are poured.
>
> This means that a greatly enhanced power of recording the

impressions of these senses and of profiting by experience—in other words, an enormous expansion of the powers of discrimination based upon acquired knowledge—is the fundamental distinction between Primitive Man and the Apes. (1924, 63)

Having already operated on the limbs to effect the transformation from monkey to ape, and before that on the eye muscles to effect the transformation from prosimian to monkey, the donor now operates on the muscles associated with articulate speech, the larynx and tongue, to effect the full transformation from ape to human. Like all such transformations, this one occurs gradually. "While still in the simian stage of development Man's ancestors were already equipped with all the specialized muscles needed for articulate speech and the cerebral apparatus for controlling their movements, and for acquiring the skill to learn new methods of action. All that was needed to put this complicated machinery to the new purpose was Man's enhanced powers of discrimination" (64). The donor's power, which is now manifest in the ability to discriminate—to *see* the difference between things—is contingent; it is

> dependent on certain cortical developments which did not occur until Man's immediate ancestors were assuming human qualities. The attainment of the realization of space and time, and a tremendous increase of range and precision in recognizing objects by their shape, colour, size, and texture, marked the transformation of the Ape into a Man. For the ability to appreciate the manifold qualities and distinctive differences made it biologically useful for him to devise names for things, and so initiated the development and use of language with all that language implies in vastly increased capacity for thinking in symbols of value to himself and intelligible to others. (152)

The power of discrimination "initiates" language and, hence, the transformation from ape to man. Once again, the donor benefits from its own actions. Language begins with naming, and according to Elliot Smith, "names were invented, at first by the definition of a visual experience." By enabling man to define visual experiences and, thus, to make them known to those who have not seen them with their own eyes, the power of vision extends its range beyond the immediately visible.

Despite this transformation, the first human is outwardly little changed from his ancestors. "Man at first, so far as his general appearance and 'build' are concerned was merely an Ape with an overgrown brain" (68). "But in virtue of those changes which convert the Ape into Man, his powers of adaptation to changes of country, climate, and food were enormously increased, so that he was able to spread abroad more quickly and roam into climates and into lands which were closed to the tropical dwelling Anthropoid Apes. Thus Man was able to make his way into every region of the earth" (63). At this stage, man differs from the ape in his body and brain, but beneath the surface, there is a more subtle distinction: he is free, whereas the ape is fettered. This distinction is reinforced in the following passage. "Man's heightened powers of discrimination and adaptation made it possible for him to extend his wanderings into all kinds of country and climate, whereas the Ape was tied down to forests and tropical temperatures" (62).

In leaving the trees, man escapes the stagnancy of the apes and, at the same time, increases the pace of his own evolution. "When man was first evolved the pace of evolution must have been phenomenally rapid, by reason of the rapid weeding-out of those who were not fleet of foot and nimble witted to meet the dangerous new conditions" (1913a, ix). Once again, Elliot Smith does not elaborate these dangerous conditions. Land bridges, avenues of opportunity, are the most conspicuous feature in Elliot Smith's terrestrial landscape.

Unhampered by tribal boundaries, Elliot Smith's terrestrial realm appears more open than those of Keith and Darwin. However, their terrestrial settings promoted a different process of evolution. In Keith's tale, tribal boundaries promote isolation and thus are a species-building force; in Darwin's, they are a means of raising the level of intratribal competition, and hence of humanity. In Elliot Smith's account, on the other hand, such boundaries are a counterproductive force, for they lead to a settling down and thus to specialization. The Law of the Unspecialized requires Elliot Smith to downplay tribal boundaries if man is to progress, just as Keith is required by his principle of segregation to emphasize them. In the next episode, we will see how tribes, with their customs and rules, constrain men—in body and mind. At this early stage, however, tribal boundaries might enhance the evolutionary process: by tempting individuals to remain within the safety of the troop, they separate the laggards from the restless.

By the beginning of the Pliocene, as Elliot Smith describes, a whole variety of "caricatures of men" are roaming across the Old World. Elliot Smith's sketches of the first members of our family— *Pithecanthropus, Sinanthropus, Eoanthropus*—do resemble caricatures: distorted human likenesses with features that are either too big or too little. Along with "the defective prefrontal and parietal areas" of the brain of *Pithecanthropus,* seen in the last episode, "there is a very pronounced local growth of the posterior part of the second temporal convolution."

> The disproportionate and precocious overgrowth of the temporal area must be regarded as the tangible evidence of the sudden increase of the importance of acoustic symbolism, which can have no meaning other than the inference that some sort of speech had been acquired by this most primitive and earliest known member of the human family. The widening of the brain in the posterior temporal area gives the primitive brain its most distinctive feature. The other point of interest . . . is the fact that the marked asymmetry of the brain, which is peculiar to the human family, is already defined. (1926, 295)

Piltdown Man, despite the already mentioned deficiencies and overgrowths of his brain, also possesses this marked asymmetry. As we have already seen, Keith had a different interpretation: he believed the two halves of the Piltdown brain were equal in size and therefore that in profile the skull should appear symmetrical. Though Elliot Smith does not name Keith in his discussion of Piltdown in *The Evolution of Man,* he addresses him directly in a 1913 letter to the journal *Nature*, in which he provides a drawing—at Keith's request—of his reconstruction of the Piltdown brain cast.

> But Prof. Keith will object that [my reconstruction] will not bring the two halves of the lambdoid suture . . . into symmetrical positions. In answer to this criticism it may be said that the lambdoid suture in this restoration is as nearly symmetrical as it is in many ancient and modern skulls. Moreover, in the case under consideration there is the most positive evidence of a lack of complete symmetry. Not only is there the most striking asymmetry in the whole occipital area . . . , but the remains of the lambdoid suture itself present a marked contrast on the two sides, being quite simple on the left, but complex and dentate on the right. (1913b, 319)

Keith and Elliot Smith are in closer agreement over the interpretation of the jaw found with the Piltdown skull fragments. "There is definite internal evidence that the jaw is not really an ape's; the teeth it bears are human, and the skull, although human, is much more primitive than any skull assigned to the genus *Homo*. This association of skull and jaw is precisely of the kind which on *a priori* grounds we should expect in an ancestral type of man" (viii). Piltdown Man fit Elliot Smith's expectations even more closely than Keith's, for as we have seen, Keith believed that "our teeth and our posture were evolved at a stage when our brain . . . had passed through only the earlier stages of development," whereas Elliot Smith believed that "the brain led the way" in human evolution. In fact, Elliot Smith has even been accused of perpetrating the hoax to confirm his views and to rile the British scientific establishment (Millar, 1972). As suggested in the opening to this chapter, this is unlikely for reasons that may be adduced from his biographies and from his own scientific writing. As Elliot Smith observes in the passage above, the Piltdown skull is "much more primitive than any assigned to the genus *Homo*." It is unlikely that he would have made such a claim, and that he would have reconstructed the skull to be so small, if he knew that it belonged to a modern human. It is also doubtful that he would have defended his reconstruction with such zeal had he known himself to be in such error.

Despite its humanlike features—and "it is almost certain that man began to speak when his jaw was in the stage represented in that of Eoanthropus" (1913a, ix)—Piltdown man is not assigned the role of hero in Elliot Smith's narrative. Though asymmetrical, its brain is too small. "It is thus definitely well below the average size of the human brain, though well within the range of its variation. But its chief interest lies not simply in its small size, but in the relatively poor development of the three areas [parietal, temporal and frontal] of chief significance" (1924, 67). Elliot Smith's rejection of Piltdown as direct ancestor may also have to do with its geographical location. Though the "highway to man's estate" circles the globe, the gateway to civilization lies, as we will shortly see, in Egypt. In contrast to his English peers, the Australian-born Elliot Smith dismisses Piltdown man as a direct human ancestor precisely because he is an Englishman and not an Egyptian.

Looking ahead to this next chapter in Elliot Smith's tale, we can see that even there fossils fall short in the area of brain development. Though the brain of Rhodesian man, a primitive member of the genus *Homo* discovered in 1921, is large in overall size, "there are still territories in the upper parietal, prefrontal, and inferior temporal regions of the Rhodesian brain which are singularly ill-developed as compared with the corresponding parts of the brains of either the Neanderthal or the modern species of Man. . . . This brain, in fact was deficient in those parts by which the degrees of foresight, discrimination, and refinement of modern men is determined and made possible" (86).

Even the brain of Neanderthal, "in which the great deficiencies found in [Rhodesian man] have been partially filled up," is lacking in its prefrontal area. In fact, Elliot Smith attributes the demise of Neanderthal man to his deficient prefrontal. "However large the brain may be in *Homo neanderthalensis*, his small prefrontal region is sufficient evidence of his lowly state of intelligence and reason for his failure in the competition with the rest of mankind" (35). Even this large brain appears lopsided and distorted:

The development of the brain of Neanderthal Man was partial and unequal. That part of the organ which plays the outstand-

ing part in determining mental superiority was not only relatively, but actually, much smaller than it is in *Homo sapiens*. The
large size of the Neanderthal brain was due to a great development of that region which was probably concerned primarily
with the mere recording of the fruits of experience, rather than
with the acquisition of great skill in the use of the hand and the
attainment of the sort of knowledge that comes from manual
experiment. (70)

Neanderthal is unbalanced and overgrown not just in his brain
but in his body.

His short, thick-set, and coarsely built body was carried in a
half-stooping slouch upon short, powerful, and half-flexed legs
of peculiarly ungraceful form. His thick neck sloped forward
from the broad shoulders to support the massive flattened head,
which protruded forward, so as to form an unbroken curve of
neck and back, in place of the alternation of curves which is one
of the graces of the truly erect *Homo sapiens*. The heavy over-
hanging eyebrow-ridges and retreating forehead, the great coarse
face with its large eye-sockets, broad nose, and receding chin,
combined to complete the picture of unattractiveness, which it is
more probable than not was still further emphasized by a shaggy
covering of hair over most of the body. The arms were relatively
short, and the exceptionally large hands lacked the delicacy and
the nicely balanced co-operation of thumb and fingers which is
regarded as one of the most distinctive of human characteristics.
(69–70)

Like the first mammals who went the way of all flesh, Neanderthal
succumbs to the temptation to specialize: "this peculiar type of mankind had in certain respects become so highly specialized as to make
it impossible to regard him as the ancestor of men of our own type"
(1928b, 113). Though Elliot Smith does not describe the benefits
conferred by his specialized body and brain—and it is unclear how
exactly he survived on the open plain—Neanderthal is "clearly
on a lower plane than its successors whom it is customary to in-

clude within the genus *sapiens*." In time, "the more nimble-witted
Homo sapiens replaced the inferior type of *Homo neanderthalensis*,
whose mere brute-strength was not sufficient to protect him from
extinction" (1924, 95).

From the motley fossil crew, one exemplar finally emerges as the
new incarnation of the hero. Cro-Magnon man stands apart from
Neanderthal man much as the first primate stood apart from the
overgrown mammals: with a "high-domed and well-filled brain"
(1926, 299) and relatively unspecialized body. The descendants of a
yet more primitive parent stock which evolved in either Asia or Africa, "the arrival in Europe of these men of modern type ought
surely to be regarded as the greatest event in [human] history," (1916,
325) for it signifies the dawn of a new age:

> The great cultural break in Western Europe itself (and even in its
> flint work) did not fall between the so-called Palaeolithic and
> Neolithic Ages, but between the Lower and the Upper Palaeolithic
> Periods.
>
> There is a much closer kinship between the flintwork of the
> so-called Upper Palaeolithic and the Neolithic Ages than there is
> between the former and that of the Lower Palaeolithic Period.
>
> Not only so, but a whole series of other industries of the
> Upper Palaeolithic Period, new methods of stone work, model-
> ling, painting, and other kinds of artistic work, reveal the mod-
> ern spirit of Man in a manner which is unknown in the Lower
> Palaeolithic. But what is more important still, men of the mod-
> ern type, undoubted members of our own species, *Homo sapi-*
> *ens*, came upon the scene in the Aurignacian Period (the com-
> mencement of the Upper Palaeolithic), and replaced *Homo*
> *neanderthalensis* of the Mousterian Period.
>
> Thus the new spirit of Man and modern Man himself are
> revealed in the Upper Palaeolithic Period. This *Neoanthropic*
> *phase*, as I have called it begins in the Aurignacian Period and
> includes all the subsequent epochs of Man's history. (1924, 90)

Elliot Smith uses the term "Neoanthropic phase" to emphasize our
own kinship with Cro-Magnon man and to separate us from the

"repellent and unattractive Neanderthal" of the preceding "Paleo-anthropic" (which includes the Chellean, Acheulean, and Mousterian cultures). He appeals to our ancestral pride in describing the industries of this phase, and yet as we will see, Cro-Magnon man's flintwork is double-edged and its cut is not liberating: the "Neoanthropic phase" signifies the New Age of Man but it, in turn, gives rise to the "Neolithic," which marks the period of man's downfall.

CIVILIZATION: in which (8) *the hero struggles* "against the forces of cultivated prejudice and inherent stupidity"; his (9) *triumph* over the "tyranny of tradition" is but a fleeting victory.

Despite his heightened mental powers and his ability to appreciate the manifold qualities of things the hero on the brink of civilization gives the impression of a single-minded creature.

> In the early days of Man's existence, when his whole attention was concentrated in satisfying his immediate appetites, he became the most expert tracker and the most acute observer of certain aspects of natural phenomena around him. In other words, he was possessed of the powers of pursuit and cunning with which all the higher Mammals are endowed, but in an immeasurably keener and subtler degree. In pursuit of his quarry and in the avoidance of danger the hunter was forced to be an observer of certain things, and was quite oblivious of others which did not affect, or did not seem to affect, his occupation. (119)

This early hunter's whole mentality is predicated on his powers of observation. He is not merely possessed of these powers, he is defined by them: he is an "acute observer." Hunting requires not only a honing of his already keen sense of sight, but also a focusing of his powers of discrimination; he must observe certain things and be oblivious to others which do not affect his occupation.

In taking up his new career, the hero appears to reach evolutionary maturity, for hunting requires not only a focusing but also a commitment to a particular occupation. Yet this new hunting way of life draws out a new mental ability, the power of causal inference.

The hero during his primitive hunting phase learns to draw links between cause and effect as skillfully as he once learned to move among branches:

> primitive natives point out the footsteps of any number of people, enumerating men, women, and children, and even their racial peculiarities and personal idiosyncracies, and will state the day or even the hour at which they passed. To the European who can detect nothing at all, or, at most, faint and confused marks, such powers seem to be almost magical. But it must be remembered that the acquisition of these powers of observation and inference occupy the whole time and attention of Primitive Man. . . . While the children of civilized Man are engaged in absorbing the fruits of their people's conventions and traditions, those of the untutored savage are acquiring the more vital knowledge of the untamed world of Nature. Each of them, and especially the latter, gives little or no thought to the contemplation of the real significance of natural phenomena. Only a very rare genius amongst either group appreciates the fact that there may be something behind the obvious veil which the majority of his fellows is accustomed to regard as the real world. (119–200)

Primitive man sees the world more clearly than we, but there is one who sees more than his fellows: the "rare genius." Unusually perceptive—it is he who sees beyond the "obvious veil" to the "real significance of things"—the rare genius possesses another extraordinary talent: the power of invention. Elliot Smith calls him the "visionary," the "man of insight." He is not merely the carrier of the donor's power, he is the donor personified. Just as the power of vision aroused new powers in the hero's brain, it is the genius who opens man's eyes to new practices. But it is a slow awakening, as Elliot Smith describes in the following passage.

> In the early history of the gropings after new knowledge and skill in arts and crafts human nature was probably not very different from what it is to-day. When, after countless thousands of years' experience of the use of stones as implements, some man

of clearer insight learned to appreciate the fact that an edge could be given to the stone by deliberately chipping it in a particular way, no doubt he was regarded as a foolish visionary, whose pretensions were resented by his staider and duller companions. Perhaps he was even reproved with the palaeolithic argument that his predecessors found unchipped stones good enough for them, and it was therefore supremely foolish to attempt to supersede methods which experience had shown to be so efficient. However, in course of time, the momentous invention was adopted: but although there are scores of ways of chipping a stone implement, the one original method was meticulously followed for many centuries to the exclusion of all others. Not only so, but it became stereotyped and adopted far and wide as one people after another learned the technique of this particular method. After this process had been going on for many centuries some new genius arose, and although no Samuel Smiles has put on record the difficulties he had to overcome before he could persuade his generation to adopt a slightly different method of chipping flint, there can be no reasonable doubt that his experience was similar to Galileo's, Watt's, and Lister's. He had to fight against the forces of cultivated prejudice and inherent stupidity. In time, however, the new technique became the fashion; and in the course of centuries it slowly percolated to the end of the earth. (103–04)

It was vision—a property of the species—that guided the hero into the trees and back down to the ground; it is the visionary who guides humankind into the Palaeolithic, but with much greater difficulty. Whereas man's remote arboreal ancestors were easily lured, primitive man must be coaxed—into the Neolithic, the Iron Age, and all the successive stages of civilization. Whereas Darwin's inventor is promptly copied by his tribe, Elliot Smith's genius must struggle against "the forces of cultivated prejudice and inherent stupidity." Civilization spreads by the slow diffusion of inventions within and between conservative tribes, rather than by the survival of tribes with inventive and imitative members, as in Darwin's story. "Such being the case, and recognizing that this complex confection was built up laboriously and exceedingly slowly, the acquisition of such arbitrary practices must be assigned to the category of knowledge that is adopted from the community in which one is born or by intimate contact with some other community which is addicted to such procedures. There is no natural impulse in Man to invent such customs or ability to do so independently in one generation" (121–22).

Like Keith, Elliot Smith depicts civilization as an unnatural state: it spreads like a disease, by intimate contact and addiction. And yet the genius, whose inventions advance this spread, is depicted as a hero. He fights against dark forces and has difficulties to overcome. Furthermore, he is embarked on a "Life Quest." When the first man of insight begins to examine the conditions of his own life, he is "actuated" by a conscious desire to overcome the greatest obstacle of all: his own mortality. In contrast to the pursuit of quarry and avoidance of danger which occupies his peers, his chief concern is to outwit death itself. His pursuit, conducted as a "quest for the elixir of life," begins with the worship of symbols of the hunt, such as blood and vital organs, and eventually extends to fertility symbols, such as cowrie shells, gold, and female figures. Of these, "the search for gold has been the most potent influence in the development of civilisation" (1923, 441). As revealed by the discovery of Tutankhamen's tomb, with its vast quantities of gold, "it was the arbitrary value attached to [gold] for its supposed magical properties that initiated the world-wide search for it which has now lasted for sixty centuries" (1923, 441). The arbitrary value attached to gold initiates more than a worldwide search for gold, it initiates also the spread of arbitrary values: of ready-made customs and beliefs which, for Elliot Smith, are the dark side of civilization.

Yet the rise of civilization hinges on specific technological practices associated with such customs and beliefs. This working hinge, which opens the gateway to civilization itself, is to be found in Egypt.

The specific activities of the embalmer who preserved the bodies of the dead were in large measure responsible for giving civilisation its distinctive character. The man who dissected the human body for the practical purpose of preventing it from suffering corruption had a much more ambitious aim than the mere preservation of a corpse. Musing deeply on the problems of life and death, he persuaded himself that in making a mummy he was actually prolonging the existence of the body so that it might be reanimated as a living being. Hence around the mummy were created, not only many of the essential arts and crafts (architecture, stone and wood-working, sculpture and painting, the drama, dancing and music) that represent the scaffolding of civilisation, but also the deepest aspirations of the human spirit, the motives which have influenced the thoughts and actions of countless millions of human beings throughout the whole history of civilisation. (1929, xv–xvi)

Civilization is built like an Egyptian tomb for the purpose of extending life beyond death. "It would, in fact, not be an exaggeration to claim that civilisation was evolved out of man's endeavours to understand the constitution of his own body and to preserve the life that animated it" (xvi–xvii). The embalmer to whom Elliot Smith traces the origins of civilization is a foreshadowing of Elliot Smith himself, the anatomical genius on his quest for the source and meaning of human existence.

Mummification gives rise to a "scaffolding" of new practices and ideas, but it rests on an earlier and even more momentous invention: agriculture. As in Keith's narrative, the invention of agriculture entails a revolutionary change, not only in the hero but in the invisible forces which control him. Whereas for Keith the shift in the balance of power between nature and civilization entails the hero's physical decline, for Elliot Smith it engenders mental disorder.

There are reasons for believing that men were, on the whole, peaceful and happy until the device of agriculture was invented. . . . For the custom of tilling the soil brought many things in its train, good and bad. It created the assurance of a food supply and a really settled mode of life, and the need (and the opportunity for satisfying it) for many arts and crafts—houses to store grain, pots for holding and cooking grain, works of irrigation for cultivating barley, and eventually the emergence of a leader to organize the community's labour and the equable distribution of water for irrigation. Weaving, the use of clothing, amulets, jewelry, the arts of the carpenter, the stonemason, the boat-builder, to mention only a few, created a division of labour, and contributed to the emergence of classes, which still further emphasized the position of the irrigation-engineer, who became the first of a dynasty of hereditary kings, the regulators of irrigation and the astronomers, who controlled their people's destiny. For the celestial phenomena they interpreted and, so to speak, made their own were regarded not merely as the measures of time and the controllers of the waters of irrigation, but also as the forces that controlled the lives of, and the processes of life-giving in, men themselves. These were the sort of circumstances that put the labour of the community at the service of one man, and conferred supernatural powers on him. Thus were created the social inequalities and the material factors that excited greed, envy and jealousy. Out of such events emerged the social organization that regulated marriage and provoked quarrelling and malicious violence. By putting power into the hands of a ruler this train of events made it possible for him not only to use the labour of the community for his own purposes, but also to exercise the power of life and death over his subjects. (1927a, 33–35)

The custom of tilling the soil ties men down, as the forest habit fetters the chimp and gorilla. Like the ape's arboreal "land of plenty which encouraged indolence in habit and stagnation of effort and growth," agriculture creates "the assurance of a food supply and a really settled mode of life." It entails also a new form of specialization: the division of labor. By creating the need for permanent shelters, water-supplies, and storage pots, agriculture transforms men into carpenters, irrigation engineers, and potters. By creating property, agriculture creates social classes. Agriculture invents men just as once it was invented by them. But it, in turn, is overpowered by one of its own inventions: the hereditary ruler. It is he who commands the tilling of the soil and its associated arts and crafts. Indeed, it is he who commands the embalmer's invention. The life the embalmer preserves is not his own but that of the king and his family.

In death, as in life, the ruler lies at the center of civilization. He is the "life-giver" of civilization, for it is he who decides who shall live and die. With his appearance, the inventive genius is displaced from his leading role: by commanding invention, the ruler invents. (In fact, the first king was an irrigation engineer in his own person.) The donor's power, earlier vested in the genius, now passes to the "hereditary king." He "excites" feelings and thoughts in his subjects, just as vision awakened new mental faculties. As vision cultivated muscular skill for its own ends, so too the ruler uses "the labour of the community for his own purposes." But whereas vision protected the hero from physical specialization, the ruler limits men to specialized forms of labor. Whereas vision awakened the mind, the ruler weakens it with fear, greed, and envy. The power to see and understand nature for oneself was the basis of mind, but the ruler undermines this power with dictates and a "ready-made supply of opinions and ways of thinking." More stultifying even than the ready-made supply of food is the "tyranny of tradition" that agriculture produces.

> The great factor in all human history has been determined by the consideration that each individual has not really had to work out his own salvation. There has been accumulating throughout the ages a body of arts and crafts, and customs and beliefs, from which each group of human beings has adopted its social equipment. For every human being there has been provided a ready-made supply of opinions and ways of thinking and acting; and in the vast majority of cases these have been accepted without question as proper and natural to accept at their face value. (1924, 134)

Inhibited from exercising the power to see for himself, the hero undergoes his final and perhaps most profound transformation. For Elliot Smith, the difference between primitive and civilized man is as great as the difference between ape and human. "Natural Man is revealed to us as a merry and good-natured fellow, honest and considerate, chaste and peaceful, with a rich imagination and a fine sense of pictorial art and craftmanship" (1927a, 30). Unlike Civilized man, he has no need of houses or clothes, nor does he display any desire to till the soil or domesticate animals. "He has no social organization apart from the family, and no hereditary chiefs. He has no property, and all the food he collects belongs to the family group. He is monogamous. He is a naked, harmless, truthful, overgrown child, kind-hearted, but quick and able to defend himself, and to stop quarrelling among his fellows" (30).

The Punans of Borneo are the ostensible model for natural man. But for Elliot Smith, as for Rousseau or Swift, it is civilized man who is the real subject and natural man is constructed as his opposite. Natural man has everything that civilized man lacks: "no property," "no social organization," and no hereditary rulers. These "negatives" are positive blessings. Possessed only of his natural powers of observation and inference, primitive man is richer than his civilized counterpart. Living without the comforts of civilization, primitive man dwells in a more vital place: "the untamed world of Nature." Elliot Smith describes this dwelling as a "Garden of Eden" and a "Golden Age of Peace and Happiness";[5] these terms describe primitive man's mind, as well as his habitat. Peace and happiness are mental states. In contrast, the mind of civilized man, like the body of Keith's modern man, exhibits multiple pathologies: overrun by "strife and discontent, dishonesty and greed, envy, malice, and all uncharitableness" (30). Overgrown by the rotting "fruits of conventions and traditions," civilization is itself a place of decay in which man, lacking the power to see for himself, wanders blindly.

Like Huxley's walled garden, civilization is presented as the antithesis of the untamed world of nature, but for Elliot Smith the ethos is reversed: the untamed world stands for good, whereas civilization is corrupt. He describes it as an "accident" and a "mistake," as though it could have been averted. Yet despite its artificial

5. Elliot Smith undertook his 1927 Conway Memorial Lecture to demonstrate the truth of Hesiod's myth of a Golden Age and Rousseau's conception of "the gentle and noble savage."

character, civilization is shown to be the almost inevitable outcome of a natural principle: "the steady and uniform development of the brain along a well-defined course." With the rise of civilization, the power of the ruler is gradually superseded by the "tyranny of tradition," and mind, now disembodied altogether, triumphs over material principles.

Elliot Smith seems to present the evolution of the brain with an eye to explaining the rise of civilization. "It is important not to forget that Man has been a wanderer ever since he came into existence and that a diffusion of culture has been effected by this means ever since he set out from his original tropical home" (1924, 63). Elliot Smith puts the cart of civilization before the horse in his description of man's wanderings out of the jungle. The teleological pull of Elliot Smith's own situation, as a twentieth-century scientist, may be felt even earlier in the story. The qualities of observation and experimentation that are cultivated in the arboreal realm are precisely those which reach fruition in that most civilized place: the scientific laboratory.

"The highway to man's estate," followed in Elliot Smith's tale, leads also to Elliot Smith's situation in post-war Europe. Elliot Smith ends his story like Keith by drawing lessons from the past that he applies to the Great War of 1914–18. "In spite of the events of ten years ago, an undoubted amelioration of the conditions of civilized life and elimination of its cruelties and hardships is in progress, even if we are still far from a Golden Age. But the realization of the innate goodness of man and the malleability of human character should eliminate the misuse of the term 'human nature' as a symbol of quarrelsomeness, and give us hope for the possibility of a progressive bettering of human conditions" (42).

Unlike Keith for whom the Great War was a natural consequence of the tribal machinery planted in the mind of man, Elliot Smith tries to see it as an artificial and contingent outgrowth of civilization. "Analysing the conditions under which these most primitive types of warfare enter into early society, like the serpent into the Garden of Eden, it becomes abundantly clear that the introduction of a class system and chieftainship was mainly responsible for the trouble" (1927, 31–33). He ends on an optimistic note by invoking the natural goodness of man, just as Darwin appeals to sympathy, "the noblest part of our nature." But the real hope for man's future lies, as in the past, with the donor. Once again, the narrator summons this "controlling power." "The complex machinery of civilization, to the use of which we are all committed, however much we may disclaim its thralldom, needs for its smooth working a controlling power that is itself disciplined and not subject to the gusts of passion to which ignorance and superstition (and, in particular, the lack of the rational judgement of an enlightened individual) expose it" (40–41).

The donor, this time in the form of an "enlightened" ruler, is to be humanity's savior. Elliot Smith is optimistic that such a donor has already answered the call and is working its magical transformation. "I should be failing in the courage of my convictions if I neglected to give expression to the belief that the system of government under which it is our good fortune to live in the British Empire offers the best opportunity for the fuller development of these principles of justice and sympathetic toleration that constitute the chief hope for the future amelioration of society" (45).

In closing, Elliot Smith himself appears an enlightened leader. As one of his biographers describes, "Elliot Smith's personal achievements stand in the records of biology. Yet undoubtedly his greater memorial is his revolutionary influence upon the course and future development of the science he loved so well. He has been accorded therefore his rightful due—an honoured place in the pantheon of British anatomists" (Cave 1938, 202). Yet there is an irony to Elliot Smith's achievement: Though he struggled—like Galileo, Lister, and Watt—against conventional beliefs, his ideas have in their turn become part of the "tyranny of tradition." Like his old rival Keith, he is remembered as an old authority rather than a young revolutionary.

Elliot Smith and Keith are meant to play a more constructive role in the narrative of this book. The purpose of the past two chapters has been to reveal the originality and complexity of their views. In the next section, their theories provide a reflective mirror with which we may recognize old beginnings, middles, and endings in recent theories of human evolution.

Part III

Contemporary Archetypes

IN 1937, the year Elliot Smith died, a book appeared that would transform the study of human evolution. *Genetics and the Origin of Species*, published when its author Theodosius Dobzhansky was only thirty-seven years old, has been called the twentieth-century counterpart to Darwin's *The Origin of Species* (Ayala 1977, 3). As the title suggests, it was "dedicated to a discussion of the mechanisms of species formation in terms of the known facts and theories of genetics." Building on the work of early-twentieth-century geneticists, Dobzhansky—who was a biologist by training—clarified the genetic causes of variability which had eluded Darwin (and also Keith and Elliot Smith) and demonstrated the relationship between these random genetic processes, such as mutation and recombination, and the process of natural selection.

The "Modern Synthesis," as the genetic theory of evolution set forth in Dobzhansky's book is now called, established natural selection as the primary creative force in evolution, by showing how adaptations could be shaped through the differential survival of random genetic variations. It also established the young Dobzhansky as one of the most influential biologists of his generation. Dobzhansky inspired colleagues in many fields to consider the problems of biology from the viewpoint of the synthesis of genetics and evolutionary theory. Works by Ernst Mayr, George Gaylord Simpson, and Julian Huxley (grandson of Thomas Henry Huxley), influenced in turn a new generation of paleoanthropologists, including J. T. Robinson, P. V. Tobias, and Sherwood Washburn. In retrospect, the publication of Dobzhansky's book in 1937 signals the dawning of a new era exceeding even the one envisioned by Darwin in *The Descent of Man*—an age in which it would be thought "wonderful" that naturalists should have doubted not only that humans evolved but that they evolved *by natural selection*.

Like Darwin, Dobzhansky addressed the question of human evolution in a separate book, *Mankind Evolving* (1962), though he had touched on it a year earlier in a paper entitled "Man and Natural Selection." The fact of human evolution was no longer in doubt. Still, some wondered whether it had been a success story.

> This has sometimes been questioned, I suspect without too much conviction on the part of the doubters, perhaps only to mock man's pretensions or to challenge his values. But man is the most successful product of evolution, by any reasonable definition of biological success. Man began his career as a rare animal, living somewhere in the tropics or subtropics of the Old World, probably in Africa. From this obscure beginning, mankind multiplied to become one of the most numerous mammals, for there will soon be about three billion men living. Numbers may not be an unadulterated blessing, but they are one of the measures of biological success of a species.
>
> Moreover, man has spread and occupied all the continents and most islands, except for the frozen wastes of Antarctica and of the interior of Greenland; he has learned to traverse seas and oceans and deserts; he is well on the way towards control or elimination of the predators and parasites which used to prey on him; he has subdued and domesticated many animal and plant species, made them serve his needs and his fancies, broadened enormously the range of utilizable food supplies, and learned to

make use of a variety of energy sources. Modern man lives no
longer at the mercy of wild beasts and vagaries of the climate; he
has reached a status where his continuation as a species is in no
danger except perhaps as a result of man's own folly or of a
cosmic accident. (1961, 285)

In fact, Dobzhansky was hopeful that in man biological evolution
had transcended itself to a new realm of self-consciousness. His
passage reflects his optimistic point of view and, at the same time,
suggests a more general perspective: a theory of human evolution
based on the principle of natural selection (which takes adversity as
the basic condition of life) conveys, even more vividly than the non-
Darwinian accounts of Keith and Elliot Smith in which the hero
leads a more sheltered life, the essence of a hero story—transformation *through struggle.*

The purpose of this section is to evoke the hero story pattern
from recent Darwinian accounts of human evolution. The aim is to
show how new fossil discoveries have been interpreted in the light of
old narratives.

Though the Piltdown forgery was not exposed until 1953, the
discovery of new fossils, and especially of more Australopithecines,
had already pushed Piltdown off most phylogenetic trees. *Australopithecus africanus*, discovered by Raymond Dart in 1925 and rejected as a hominid by many paleoanthropologists, including Arthur Keith, now occupied a more central position. Robert Broom's
discovery in 1936 of more specimens of *Australopithecus africanus*,
and twelve years later of a related species now known as *Australopithecus robustus*, convinced many paleoanthropologists (including
Keith) that *Australopithecus africanus* was not only a hominid but a
direct human ancestor. It is only in recent years that its ancestral
status has been threatened, first by the discovery of *Homo habilis* in
1961 and *Australopithecus afarensis* in 1974. This "threat" has been
met by an attempt to vindicate *Australopithecus africanus* and re-
store it to a central role in human evolution.

By looking at the key papers in the history of this debate, one
can pick out a set of themes which echo the literary archetype of

"the mysterious birth."[1] In many stories, the hero is born in obscurity or is cast out into the world soon after birth and spends his youth unaware of his true parentage. In some stories, this beginning sets the agenda for the rest of the tale: the hero must discover his true identity. This search is associated with a variety of themes. For example, often the hero is born under unusual circumstances or with special powers or charms. These special powers, which set the hero apart during his youth, enable him to discover his true origins when he reaches manhood. This knowledge, in turn, liberates him to inherit a kingdom, marry, or otherwise achieve his own destiny.

The archetype of the mysterious birth is seen most clearly in the search for the "missing link"—the long-lost ancestor of humans. It may also be used to highlight a set of themes found in recent paleo-anthropological writing. These discussions have tended to stress the uniqueness of man and have pointed out that his emergence from a prehuman state involved unusual circumstances (Goudge 1961, 133). The course of evolution since his emergence is seen to be determined by new factors of a nonbiological kind: man himself began to produce a new set of causal factors and thereby initiated a new kind of evolution. Finally, it is believed that an understanding of these factors will enable modern man to direct his own evolution.

Though these may be verifiable contentions, they far exceed what can be inferred from the study of fossils alone and in fact place a heavy burden of interpretation on the fossil record—a burden which is relieved by placing fossils into preexisting narrative structures. The fossil record itself may gain much of its aura of self-evidence from the incantatory authority of the ancient narrative structures it follows.

I have said earlier that what distinguishes recent accounts from

1. Frye defines archetype in *The Anatomy of Criticism:* "Archetypes are associative clusters. . . . Within the complex is often a large number of specific learned associations which are communicable because a large number of people in a given culture happen to be familiar with them" (1957, 102). In *The Secular Scripture* (1976), he discusses the "motif" of mysterious birth and points out how it is often associated in the novel with other motifs, such as "the placement of birth-tokens and talismans" which are used to establish "the hero's true parentage" at the end of the story. I refer to this cluster of motifs as the "archetype" of the mysterious birth.

those of Keith and Elliot Smith is the renewed emphasis on natural selection. Though natural selection plays the role of the donor in the following accounts, it does so only up to a point. As we shall see, even Darwinians departed from Darwinian principles when explaining the later stages of human evolution.

6   Discoveries and Recoveries

Dart and the Discovery of Australopithecus africanus

THE BURDEN of interpretation, which is often manifest in an emphasis on the human features of new fossil finds, is evident in Raymond Dart's original 1925 description of the nearly complete skull of *Australopithecus africanus* discovered at Taungs, South Africa. "In the first place, the whole cranium displays *humanoid* rather than anthropoid lineaments. . . . The orbits are not in any sense detached from the forehead, which rises steadily from their margins in a fashion amazingly human. . . . The malars, zygomatic arches, maxillae, and mandible all betray a delicate and humanoid character" (1925, 195–96).

Keith, as we recall, rejected *Australopithecus africanus* as a hominid because he could not see any character in the skull which justified the supposition of the erect posture, despite Dart's enumeration of such features.

That hominid characters were not restricted to the face in this primate group is borne out by the relatively forward situation of the foramen magnum. . . . [This] points to the assumption by this fossil group of an attitude appreciably more erect than that of modern anthropoids. The improved poise of the head, and the better posture of the whole body framework which accompanied this alteration . . . means that a greater reliance was being placed by this group upon the feet as organs of progression, and that the hands were being freed from their primitive function of accessory organs of locomotion. Bipedal animals, their hands were assuming a higher evolutionary role not only as delicate tactual, examining organs . . . but also as instruments of the growing intelligence in carrying out more elaborate, purposeful, and skilled movements. (197)

Dart's explanatory sequence repeats elements found in the accounts of Haeckel and Darwin, in particular, the greater reliance on the feet as organs of progression and the freeing of the forelimbs to become instruments of intelligence. He also echoes motifs introduced by his mentor Elliot Smith,[2] such as the emphasis on skilled movements. Elliot Smith's influence, in particular his belief that the brain led the way in human evolution, can also be seen in Dart's description of the Taungs endocranial cast.

Whatever the total dimensions of the adult brain may have been, there are not lacking evidences that the brain in this group of fossil forms was distinctive in type and was an instrument of greater intelligence than that of living anthropoids. . . . The brain does not show that general pre- and post-Rolandic flattening characteristic of the living anthropoids, but presents a rounded and well filled-out contour, which points to a symmetrical and balanced development of the faculties of associative memory and intelligent activity. (197)

In comparison to this shapely brain, the flattened anthropoid brain appears, like the lopsided brains of the Neanderthals in Elliot Smith's account, mentally deficient.

---

2. Dart, who was Australian, worked closely with Elliot Smith while he was a medical student in London.

Nothing could illustrate better the mental gap that exists between living anthropoid apes and the group of creatures which the fossil represents than the flattened atrophic appearance of the parietal region of the brain (which lies between the visual field on one hand, and the tactile and auditory fields on the other) in the former and its surgent vertical and dorso-lateral expansion in the latter. The expansion in this area of the brain is the more significant in that it explains the posterior *humanoid* situation of the sulcus lunatus. It indicates . . . the fact that this group of beings, having acquired the faculty of stereoscopic vision, had profited beyond living anthropoids by setting aside a relatively much larger area of the cerebral cortex to serve as a storehouse of information concerning their objective environment as its details were simultaneously revealed to the sense of vision and touch, and also of hearing. . . . In other words, their eyes saw, their ears heard, and their hands handled objects with greater meaning and fuller purpose than the corresponding organs in recent apes. They had laid down the foundation of that discriminative knowledge of the appearance, feeling, and sound of things that was a necessary milestone in the acquisition of articulate speech. (198)

The acquisition of stereoscopic vision lays the foundation for the power of discrimination, which in turn prepares the way for articulate speech, as in Elliot Smith's tale. Yet the driving force effecting the further transformation of *Australopithecus africanus* lies outside the cranial vault in the veldt of Southern Africa:

there has been a tendency to overlook the fact that, in the luxuriant forests of the tropical belts, Nature was supplying with profligate and lavish hand an easy sluggish solution, by adaptive specialisation, of the problem of existence in creatures so well equipped mentally as living anthropoids are. For the production of man a different apprenticeship was needed to sharpen the wits and quicken the higher manifestations of intellect—a more open veldt country where competition was keener between swiftness and stealth, and where adroitness of thinking and movement played a preponderating role in the preservation of the species. Darwin has said, "no country in the world abounds in a greater degree with dangerous beasts than Southern Africa," and, in my opinion, Southern Africa, by providing a vast open country with occasional wooded belts and a relative scarcity of water, together with a fierce and bitter mammalian competition, furnished a laboratory such as was essential to this penultimate phase of human evolution. (199)

Compared to the terrestrial laboratory of Elliot Smith's account—which appears more like a finishing school—the veldt is truly a "hard school of experience." With its scarcity of resources and fierce mammalian foes, the terrestrial realm is much harsher even than in *The Descent of Man*. Darwin's hero, who had his hands full fighting off his semihuman foes, could hardly have coped with an environment as hostile as Dart's Southern Africa. Dart puts man more squarely in the natural world. By depriving him for the most part of the benefits of society, he casts him as a less congenial character very early in the story. To survive such dangerous circumstances, the hero must himself be a dangerous creature.

For the first time, the moral nature of the hero is bad from the start, rather than corrupted by agricultural surplus, civilization, or superstition. As Dart relates in his classic paper "The predatory transition from ape to man" (1953),

The australopithecine deposits of Taungs, Sterkfontein and Makapansgat tell us in their way a consistent, coherent story not of fruit-eating, forest-loving apes, but of the sanguinary pursuits and carnivorous habits of proto-men. They were human not merely in having the facial form and dental apparatus of humanity; they were also human in their cave life, in their love of flesh, in hunting wild game to secure meat and in employing implements, whether wielded and propelled to kill during hunting or systematically applied to the cracking of bones and the scraping of meat from them for food. Either these Procrustean proto-human folk tore the battered bodies of their quarries limb from limb and slaked their thirst with blood, consuming the flesh raw

like every other carnivorous beast; or, like early man, some of
them understood the advantages of fire as well as the use of
missiles and clubs. (1953, 204)

In either case, they were the most savage creatures on the veldt
—crueler than even the fiercest carnivore. On the basis of several
battered Australopithecine skulls discovered at Makapansgat, Dart
concluded that our ancestors killed their own kind—a practice unknown in any other living animal but a habit all too human.

> The loathsome cruelty of mankind to man forms one of his ines-
> capable, characteristic and differentiative features; and it is ex-
> plicable only in terms of his carnivorous, and cannibalistic
> origin. . . . The blood-bespattered, slaughter-gutted archive of
> human history from the earliest Egyptian and Sumerian records
> to the most recent atrocities of the second World War accord
> with early universal cannibalism, with animal and human
> sacrificial practices or their substitutes in formalized religions
> and with the world-wide scalping, head-hunting, body-mutilating
> and necrophilic practices of mankind in proclaiming this com-
> mon bloodlust differentiator, this predaceous habit, this mark of
> Cain that separates man dietetically from his anthropoidal rela-
> tives and allies him rather with the deadliest of Carnivora.
> (207–08)

Though cannibalism is not explicitly mentioned in *The Descent
of Man*, according to Dart, "Darwin recognized this sinister aspect
of human evolution" when discussing the "strange superstitions and
customs" of savages. Dart finds further support for his view of early
man's predaceous behavior in Darwin's passage on the upright
posture: "if Darwin's reasoning was correct, man's erect posture is
the concrete expression of signal success in this type of life. It emerged
through and was consolidated by the defensive and offensive stone-
throwing and club-swinging technique necessitated by attacking and
killing prey from the standing position. . . . [T]his implies . . . the
capacity to stand still and to transform the immobilized feet into a
rock-like base from which the whirling body can operate as a whole"

(209). Whereas the trunk and arms act as a prop for the brain in Elliot Smith's account, they act here as a propeller, specialized for the purposes of killing.

> At one extreme the gibbon has specialized in whirling himself from the branches of trees; at the other extreme man has specialized in whirling the branches of the trees about himself. These bludgeon-whirling activities became significant when there was skilled work apart from tree-climbing of biological usefulness such as hunting for these competent hands to do; the seizing of victims, prey or quarry; the thirst for blood and the hankering after flesh for food; the carnivorous diet. (211).

Dart portrays the activities of our ancestors in vivid terms, but these actions are determined by the pressure of natural selection, operating through the unusually demanding veldt environment. "The habits of baboons show that the predatory tendency becomes seasonal and even systematic in a much less capable primate than *Australopithecus* in the exacting terrestrial environment of Southern Africa" (1953, 215). And yet even under the most rigorous conditions, baboons would not take to killing their own kind. Carnivores, who eat only meat, rarely resort to cannibalistic practices. In this regard, man is an anomaly.

But the circumstances surrounding his birth may appear mysterious to man for a different reason.

> From the Biblical story of the Garden of Eden to the cult of vegetarianism . . . civilized man has been steadily and increasingly separated from his carnivorous past. . . . Whether the factors relentlessly imposing a meatless existence on mankind today be ritualistic or economic, they are contrary to his original nature. They assist however in explaining the incredulity many groups of human beings share about the carnivorous phase in the transition from ape to man and the past reluctance to envisage the implications of the multimillennial proto-human and human predaceous habit for the understanding of man's essential nature. (216)

Dart intends to shock us out of our collective amnesia, just as Huxley awoke his readers from their sleep, into a recognition of the truth about our ancestry. Like the nineteenth-century discovery of the manlike apes, the discovery of *Australopithecus africanus* confirmed what had hitherto been imagined. "It is in these matters that the Taungs remains have their significance. They have rendered real what hitherto has been theoretical" (1926, 315).

Robinson and the Discovery of Australopithecus robustus

The Taungs skull provided more than a reification of preexisting beliefs; it pointed the way to new discoveries: "we may confidently anticipate many complementary discoveries concerning this period in our evolution" (315). Of these later finds, *Paranthropus* (later renamed *Australopithecus robustus*), discovered in 1948 by Robert Broom and J. T. Robinson, was the most complementary. As Robinson described, when compared to *Paranthropus* with its massive face and jaws, *Australopithecus africanus* assumed an even more humanlike appearance.

> *Australopithecus* has a dolichocephalic skull with a good hominine shape. A distinct low forehead is present, and the vertex rises well above the level of the browridges. The latter are poorly developed, and the postorbital constriction is moderately developed. . . . The skull is gracile without any heavy bone or strong development of ridges or crests.
>
> *Paranthropus* is very different. . . . The skull is brachycephalic with not a trace of a forehead; the frontal passes straight back from the well-developed supraorbital torus in a manner reminiscent of the condition in the gorilla. The vertex rises very little above the upper level of the orbits. . . . A most unusual situation exists in the dentition. (1961a, 4)

As in Keith's contrast between the overgrown Neanderthal and healthy Cro-Magnon Man, *Paranthropus* is drawn as the abnormal counterpart to the "normal" *Australopithecus*.

The dentition of *Australopithecus* is normal in the sense that the teeth are all, in size, to a matching scale. The molars are moderately large and so are the premolars and canines. But in *Paranthropus* the molars are appreciably larger than those of the latter form. This lends a very unusual appearance to the dentition, as the incisors and canines are in quite a different scale to the premolars and molars with a sharp distinction between the two groups. Such a definite difference must have some clear explanation. (1956, 168)

According to Robinson, the key difference between the two was that *Paranthropus* was a vegetarian, whereas *Australopithecus* ate meat.

The adaptive difference between these two forms is thus considerable. Their ecological requirements and direction of evolution were quite different. The degree of difference between them in these respects was of a distinctly greater order than between any two of the living pongids. . . . It is interesting to note that good evidence exists indicating that the vegetarian *Paranthropus* was present in the Sterkfontein Valley in times when the climate was apparently significantly wetter than when the more carnivorous *Australopithecus* lived there. (1961b, 484–85)

The contrast between wet and dry explains the divergence of *Paranthropus* and *Australopithecus*, just as the contrast between forests and veldt explained the divergence of humans and apes in Dart's narrative. Natural selection, operating through the dessication of the African veldt, sets the tests that separate the two and leads, eventually, to the appearance of the genus *Homo*.

It is not difficult, then, to visualize the steady but slow progress of the dessication process. After a while australopithecine groups would begin to find it less easy to survive the critical time of the year—the latter end of the dry season—because of food shortage. Under these circumstances they will almost certainly have supplemented their diet with insects, birds, reptiles, and small mammals such as rodents. As aridity increased they will have had to rely on this supplement to their diet more and more.

In some areas populations will probably have died out entirely, but it is not unreasonable, in view of known evidence of primate dietary adaptability, to suppose that some groups will have succeeded in surviving on their modified diet.

However, these changed conditions will also have modified the selection pressures operating on the population. It would seem obvious that intelligence would be at a premium since some ingenuity would be required to get enough to eat, whereas this is much less so in the case of a vegetarian living under reasonably wet conditions. The more intelligent ones would therefore be able to adapt better to the changing conditions and are likely to have been the parents of the majority of the next generation. Also, whereas the simplest tools suffice for a vegetarian and in almost all cases none at all are needed, tools would obviously be of great use to the population adapting to more arid conditions. Implements for digging animals out of holes, snares for catching prey, implements for bashing or opening up animals, would all enable far more efficient adaptation. (1961b, 493–94)

Compared to the cracking and scraping of Dart's Procrustean proto-human folk, this bashing and opening up of animals does sound more efficient. Still, it must have been a relatively crude activity as performed by *Australopithecus*. As Robinson observes, the archeological record associated with *Australopithecus* is primitive, at best:

That is to say, roughly 96 percent of the known South African material of *Australopithecus* is not associated with a stone industry, but suddenly a stone industry representing a stage near the beginnings of the Chelles-Acheul culture appears in reasonable quantity toward the end of Sterkfontein time. Where did it come from? The only reasonable conclusion seems to be that a toolmaker invaded the Sterkfontein Valley during the time represented by the unconformity—and that invader could not have been *Australopithecus* as he had already been there for a long time. (489)

A more likely candidate for the role of toolmaker had, in fact, been discovered by Robinson himself in 1949 and provisionally assigned to a new genus "Telanthropus" (later subsumed under *Homo erectus*). "It seems anything but coincidence that the stone industry appears in the Sterkfontein Valley at just about the time that the remains of 'Telanthropus' also appear there. As has been pointed out, 'Telanthropus' has some major features which can be matched only among toolmaking hominines but not among the australopithecines. What could be more logical than that it was the invading toolmaker?" (490).

Still, the question remained: How did Telanthropus acquire his toolmaking ability in the first place? This special ability did not arise, as simple tool use did in *Australopithecus*, as a response to an adverse environment.

> In this manner it [was] easy to explain the origin of *Australo-pithecus*. But once [the evolutionary] process had reached the point of producing such a creature, there is no reason at all why it should stop there. Improved intelligence and improved facility with tools would continue to improve adaptation and it would appear that sooner or later—and probably relatively soon—a stage would be reached when conceptual thought would begin to appear and tool using would improve to tool making as well. This point, of which toolmaking is, as it were, a symptom, seems a logical place to regard as that at which true man emerged. It was here that the fundamental feature of man, culture, became established. (494)

Natural selection loosens its grip with the first appearance of tool-making. Toolmaking is a natural consequence—a "symptom"—of "improved" intelligence and facility with tools, rather than the re-sult of the accidental birth of inventive individuals, as it was in the Darwinian narrative.

Unlike Darwin, who manages to keep man under selective con-trol even while he is acquiring a moral sense, Robinson leaves him more and more to his own devices.

[Man] is able to manufacture devices which enable him to go up higher or down deeper than any other creature and to penetrate climatic extremes to a degree denied any orthodox animal. In so doing he has succeeded in altering the pattern of evolution; for instance, natural selection does not operate for him in quite the same way as it does generally. . . . Now this form of mental behaviour [inventiveness] is an important human characteristic and should be taken into account. We realise full well that it is far from being well developed and that man is now in a dangerous transitional phase which, to the palaeontologist of the future, will be a fine example of quantum evolution involving a major adaptive shift through a critical phase of precarious adaptation. But the majority will agree I am sure, that the risks are worth running because of the enormous potentialities of an emancipated intelligence. (166)

Like Dobzhansky, who believed that biological evolution was transcending itself in man, Robinson interprets the recent appearance of intelligence to be a sign of its potential for further self-directed evolution. However, he is cautiously optimistic: "It is a sobering thought that the buttocks had more to do with the origin of the human line than had the brain!" (166–67). . . . though not nearly so shocking as Dart's grim conclusion.

This lesson—the priority of bipedalism—may be read in the phylogenetic tree which Robinson includes at the end of his 1961 paper, for it is the bipedal common ancestor of *Paranthropus* and *Australopithecus* who is depicted there as the very first hominid. Robinson's drawing, which he calls a "schematic representation of the relationship between *Paranthropus*, *Australopithecus*, and *Homo*," is even sketchier than the phylogenies of Elliot Smith and Keith; it does not include a time scale. Nor do any known fossil species lie on the direct human line: even *Australopithecus africanus* and *Homo erectus* occupy side branches. Like the drawings of Keith and Elliot Smith, it expresses Robinson's general understanding of human evolution—as a process of adaptive radiation, competitive exclusion, and phyletic change—rather than specific ancestor descendent sequences. Robinson recapitulates this general understand-ing in an address published in 1961:

> *Paranthropus* and *Australopithecus* . . . were divergent, adaptively well separated stocks which represented an adaptive radiation within the prehominines and could have occupied the same ter-ritory successfully for a long time. Both did in fact exist synchro-nously in Africa over a substantial period of time. . . . But *Australopithecus* and *Homo* are much more closely related and are probably two phases of the same phyletic sequence, though evidently one species of *Australopithecus* was con-temporaneous for a short time with an early *H. erectus* in the Sterkfontein Valley. This overlap in time appears to have been short; the ecological similarity between the two makes it un-likely that it could have been long anywhere. But there is no sharp discontinuity between *Australopithecus* and *Homo*—ex-cept in brain size in the known specimens. But clearly there must have been at least one line in which this gap also was bridged. (1961b, 499).

Tobias and the Discovery of Homo habilis

In fact, such a "bridge" was found that very year with Louis Leakey's discovery at Olduvai Gorge of the mandible, cranial, and postcranial fragments of a new and relatively large brained hominid. These fossil remains were placed into a new species, *Homo habilis*, in 1964 by Leakey and his colleagues Philip Tobias and John Napier—to Robinson's dismay. The Olduvai fossils were too similar to *Australopithecus africanus* to warrant the recog-nition of a new species; instead he believed that "[new specimens] represent a transitional stage between *Australopithecus* and *H. erectus* just at that stage where the essentially tool-using stage of the former was giving way to the primarily tool-making condi-tion of the latter. . . . If the interpretation suggested here is correct, clearly no new species name is needed" (Robinson 1965, 8). Robin-son suggested that even *Australopithecus* be collapsed into the genus

Homo.[3] "This genus would then include the whole sequence from the point where a shift to an omnivorous diet (by the inclusion of a substantial degree of carnivorousness) caused a new set of selection pressures to come into play favouring the whole complex of culture as a means of adaptation and thus caused the emergence of culture-bearing man" (9). Paradoxically, the new discoveries from Olduvai would bring about a reduction in the number of known hominid species.

Robinson's revision drew an immediate response from Philip Tobias, one of the namers of *Homo habilis*. Tobias's main effort was directed at showing that the Olduvai remains were much less similar to *Australopithecus africanus* than Robinson claimed, and that the discontinuity between *Homo* and *Australopithecus* was much greater.

> Although *Australopithecus* fulfills the morphological require-ments for an ancestor of man, there remains a substantial gap between the australopithecines and the most lowly representa-tive of the hominines hitherto recognized (that is, *Homo erectus*, formerly called *Pithecanthropus, Sinanthropus, Atlanthropus,* and so on). The size of this morphological gap may best be illus-trated by reference to three parameters which have shown most marked change during the process of hominization in the Pleistocene: brain size, tooth size, and tooth shape. (Tobias 1965b, 25)

Tobias, in each case, comes to the same conclusion: "there is a big-ger gap between *Australopithecus* and *Homo erectus* than between any other two consecutive groups." Tobias states this point again and again, just as Huxley repeated the main lesson, that the differ-ences between monkeys and apes are greater than between apes and humans, in *Man's Place in Nature*. Tobias investigates the three pa-rameters of brain size, tooth size, and tooth shape as Huxley stud-ied the three structures in the brain—to contradict his opponent's

---

3. Robinson divided this genus into two species: *Homo transvalensis* (includ-ing *Australopithecus africanus* and *Homo habilis*) and *Homo sapiens* "Telanthropus" (including *Homo erectus* and *Homo sapiens*).

claim (in Tobias's case, Robinson's claim that there was "insufficient morphological space") and also to make room for the new fossil. "It is this gap that has been filled by *Homo habilis*, the newly discovered hominid which, with respect to the three parameters used to characterize the gap, as well as with respect to other morphological markers, lies in a largely intermediate position" (26). *Homo habilis*, initially described as "a hitherto-unrecognized and even unsuspected transitional or intermediate form of early man," now appears an almost perfect fit for the role of human ancestor.

On the other hand, *Australopithecus africanus* seems a less likely candidate. The human aspects of its anatomy and its behavior are called into question by the recognition of *Homo habilis*.

> Dart has demonstrated that the australopithecines were capable of a wide range of cultural activities. It may, however, be argued that all of these activities fall into the categories which Napier has classified as *ad hoc* tool-using, purposeful tool-using, tool-modifying for an immediate or even for a future purpose, and possibly even *ad hoc* tool-making. But it may be questioned whether these australopithecine activities constitute cultural tool-making—that is, whether they exhibit a set and regular complex of patterns which, moreover, show developmental trends with the passage of time.
>
> If this interpretation is correct, ethological or cultural evidence could be added to the anatomical evidence which tends to ally *H. habilis* with the hominines rather than with the australopithecines. (30–31)

Homo habilis falls on the far side of the narrow but deep cultural divide which separates tool use and toolmaking. In fact, it falls into the same slot as Telanthropus, Robinson's mysterious invader. But for Tobias, the discovery of the toolmaker entails a splitting off of *Australopithecus africanus* from the direct human line rather than a bridging, as in Robinson's phylogeny. "Chronologically, the recognition of *H. habilis* means that a more hominized line of creatures was evolving alongside the somewhat less hominized australopithecines even in the Lower Pleistocene" (31). As Tobias further describes, the splitting off of the hominine line leaves *Australopithecus africanus* at the end of a "residual" lineage.

The ancestral australopithecine was unspecialized, small-toothed, omnivorous. At some time in the Upper Pliocene, it diversified into macrodontic and megadontic lines (*A. robustus* and *A. boisei*) with specialized dentition, perhaps accompanying a specialized, essentially herbivorous diet. Another line remained little changed and unspecialized, eventually to dichotomize into a progressively more hominized line represented by *H. habilis* in Africa and perhaps *Meganthropus* in Asia and a more conservative residual line (*A. africanus*) which, because of ecological similarities to *H. habilis*, did not long outlast the emergence of this hominine.

Tobias does not say here how exactly natural selection operates to bring the australopithecine line to an end. The donor of his account is rendered more vividly—as are other narrative elements—in his 1965 presidential address to the South African Archaeological Society.

The australopithecines . . . lived in a habitat providing little natural protection and they had no natural weapons of offence or defence like large canines. Their implemental activities had come to loom very largely in their pattern of adjustment. Indeed, it would not be too much to claim that their very survival depended on implemental activities. This, it is suggested, is the great step forward of the australopithecines over the apes. They learned to exploit a mental and manipulative capacity, a cultural potentiality, which even apes possess. And they exploited it so effectively that they became dependent on it for survival. Cultural capacity was the greatest evolutionary asset of the australopithecines: and it was on this aspect of their form and function that selection operated with the greatest vigour.

Small wonder then that, sooner or later, some among the numerous Africa-wide populations of australopithecines did acquire the mental capacity to overleap the highest implemental

frontier. . . . Sooner or later, some of them did acquire the right
quantity and/or quality of brain to be able to use a tool to make
a tool. Initially, perhaps this would have been an isolated flash in
the pan, but if it conferred a sufficient selective advantage, the
capacity for it would have spread. . . . This new development
clearly did not require a very much bigger brain than that possessed by *Australopithecus*—perhaps another (American) billion
nerve cells were sufficient.

Now a new major breakthrough occurred. Stone tool-making
of the complexity of an Oldowan culture became feasible: new,
virtually limitless possibilities opened up. A new kind of man
was born—*Homo habilis*—with a new set of implemental capacities, achievements and frontiers. (1965a, 189)

Humankind enters a new domain, but it does so through a
familiar-sounding passage. Tobias repeats many of the elements of
the narratives of Darwin, Dart, and even Robinson. Toolmaking
develops from tool using in an almost inevitable way, "sooner or
later," as in Robinson's account, though Tobias is more specific about
the neurobiological basis of this development. His depiction of the
hominization process as a series of "leaps forth" and "break-
throughs" ends, finally, with humans setting their own challenges,
as in Robinson's account, and even controlling the destinies of other
hominids, such as *Australopithecus robustus*, whose "over-specialized
offshoots seem to have suffered genocidal extinction in the Middle
Pleistocene. They were one of Nature's unsuccessful experiments,
like the dinosaurs. They eked out an existence here in the Transvaal,
long after more highly hominized, more competitive forms of hominid had appeared on the scene: and perhaps it was these advanced
cousins of theirs that were, in the event, responsible for their disappearance" (1965b, 32–33).

Yet Tobias does not believe that the murderous past of man is
cause for pessimism. In contrast to the final reminder of *The Descent of Man* that "Man still bears in his bodily frame the indelible
stamp of his lowly origin," Tobias ends by depicting humans as
transcendent.

Man is pre-eminent among the beasts in his degree of dependence upon cultural mechanisms for survival. As Teilhard de Chardin put it, "evolution went straight to work on the brain, neglecting everything else, which accordingly remained malleable." Somewhere, in the line of ever-warming consciousness, "a flame bursts forth at a strictly localised point. Thought is born." And this brought "an incredible commotion among the spheres of life." "Hominisation," he says, "can be accepted in the first place as the individual and instantaneous leap from instinct to thought. . . . " Thus, although the anatomical leap from non-man to man is small and insignificant, it is a change marked by the birth of a new sphere, that of thinking. With man, we have entered "the psychozoic era."

Carry this process forward and we reach a kind of climax in the last century, with the acceptance and gradual understanding of the process of evolution. In this little time, "What has made us in four or five generations so different from our forebears . . . , so ambitious, too, and so worried, is not merely that we have discovered and mastered other forces of nature. In the final analysis, it is, if I am not mistaken, that we have become conscious of the movement which is carrying us along. . . ." and therein, de Chardin echoed the concise expression of [Julian] Huxley that man has discovered *he is nothing else than evolution become conscious of itself*. (36)

So, too, Thomas Henry Huxley believed that an understanding of evolution would transform humanity. Yet he believed that man —the Alps and Andes of the world—would be "transfigured by reflecting here and there, a ray from the infinite source of truth," rather than by actually becoming that source of understanding. In fact, he and his German counterpart Haeckel waged their struggle on Darwin's behalf as part of a larger campaign to establish man's place in the material world, whereas De Chardin appears to invoke metaphysical principles with the entry into a psychozoic era. Indeed, his image of a "flame bursting forth at a strictly localised point" is reminiscent of the divine spark of the doctrine of special creation.

"As Dobzhansky pointed out, since, 'in giving rise to man, the evolutionary process has, apparently for the first and only time in the history of the Cosmos, become conscious of itself . . . this opens at least a possibility that evolution may some day be directed by man'" (40). Evolution reaches a new stage with the appearance of man; at the same time, man is presented as the embodiment of evolution. Whereas man uses his godlike power to carry out evil deeds in the narrative of Elliot Smith, Tobias emphasizes the benefits that may be conferred by humanity.

> It is well to stress these hopeful developments because, as Dobzhansky has aptly put it, "Cassandras prophesying doom attract public attention more easily than do those who hold the unspectacular view that a disaster is not around the corner, and not even inevitable."
>
> So even our physical evolution of tomorrow may be controlled by our evolution in the intellectual sphere. . . .
>
> If evolution engenders a sense of optimism for the future, such optimism stems solely from the idea that the future good in the material sense will coincide with the future good in the ethical sense. (40–43).

In sharp contrast to Huxley's walled garden in which evolution and ethics are at odds, Tobias depicts the future of human civilization as a utopian paradise:

> Whichever precise direction or even directions Man's development takes, we may be confident that it will be evolution at a new level which has set him apart from the other animals — the level of Teilhard's noosphere, of [Julian] Huxley's psychozoic realm. It is the domain not only of reason, but of birdsong and sunsets and warm eyes. As Dostoievsky put it "beauty will save the world." And didn't Keats long ago divine this when he wrote "'Beauty is truth, truth beauty, — that is all / Ye know on earth, and all ye need to know'"? Compassion and intellect are our signposts pointing to Man's long future without despair: that is the irresistible message of Yesterday's Man to the Man of Tomorrow. (41–43)

Johanson and White and the Discovery of Australopithecus afarensis

Yesterday's man might enjoin tomorrow's man to harmony and peace, but he would cause commotion among paleoanthropologists over the next decade. The discovery in 1972 at East Turkana, Kenya, of an almost complete *Homo habilis* (the famous ER 1470) skull assured that species a place in most phylogenetic trees, but it called into question the ancestral status of *Australopithecus africanus*.[4] Discoveries from Laetoli and Hadar cast further doubt on *Australopithecus africanus*, calling Tobias to its rescue.

> During the seventies, a succession of East African discoveries has been claimed to represent the "true" ancestral line of modern man, thus relegating *A. africanus* . . . to a subordinate role in hominid phylogeny. The latest such attempt has been the claim of Johanson and his co-workers that the 3.7–2.6 My-old hominids of Laetoli in Tanzania and of Hadar in Ethiopia represent a new species, "A. afarensis", which led to *H. habilis*, whilst *A. africanus* represents early stages in a specialized side-branch leading to *A. robustus* and *A. boisei*. (Tobias 1980, 1)

Like Dart's famous announcement of 1925, the description by Donald Johanson and Tim White of *Australopithecus afarensis* caused enormous debate. At issue was not only the ancestral status of the new fossil finds but Johanson and White's claim that the Hadar and Laetoli remains belonged to the same species: "the strong morphological and chronological continuity seen between the Hadar and Laetoli fossil hominid samples strongly suggests that these collections are most conveniently and effectively considered together in the following systematic assessment" (Johanson and White 1979, 321). The burden of this interpretation—that the Hadar and Laetoli remains belong to the same taxonomic group—is evident in the description of the fossils themselves. "The lower molars, particu-

4. This was because the 750 c.c skull was originally assigned a date of 2.5 million years. *Australopithecus africanus* was reinstated when the date of E.R. 1470 was revised to 1.8 m.y.

larly the first and second, *tend* to be square in outline. The cusps are *usually* arranged in a simple Y–5 pattern, surrounding wide occlusal foveae. The third molars are *generally* larger and their distal outlines are rounded. The molar sequence is *normally* M3>M2>M1. The upper molars *usually* follow the same size sequence, their occlusal foveae are wide, and their hypocones are fully developed" (322; italics mine). The Hadar and Laetoli molars are presented as "usually," "generally" or "normally" arranged, reinforcing the impression that they belong to one group. This argument is further strengthened by the linking of individual features into constellations. "The Laetoli and Hadar fossil hominid remains have a distinctive *suite of primitive cranial and postcranial characters.* . . . In summary, the Hadar and Laetoli remains seem to represent a distinctive early hominid form characterized by substantial sexual dimorphism and a *host of primitive dental and cranial characters.*" (321–25; italics mine).

The grouping of primitive traits into "suites" and "hosts" consolidates the position of *Australopithecus afarensis* as a single taxonomic group and at the same time establishes its central phylogenetic position:

> The overview of the Laetoli and Hadar remains presented above indicates that these forms represent the most primitive group of demonstrable hominids yet recovered from the fossil record. . . . They allow a perception of human evolution that was hitherto impossible. . . . To fully appreciate this new resolution of early hominid phylogeny, it is necessary to consider the historical framework of fossil hominid discoveries. This is particularly true because the recent discoveries from eastern Africa have usually been interpreted in terms of a framework formulated on the basis of the South African discoveries. (1979, 325)

Yet the phylogenetic tree presented by Johanson and White is very similar to that proposed by J. T. Robinson in 1961. The main difference is that *Australopithecus afarensis* fills the slot formerly occupied by *Australopithecus africanus.*

Johanson and White seem to recognize the similarity between

the South African framework and the apparently new resolution afforded by *Australopithecus afarensis*. "Until this species was identified, the most parsimonious interpretation of early hominid phylogeny was one where *A. africanus* represented a ' . . . "perfect ancestor" . . . ', and stood below the major fork in the hominid evolutionary tree. We now suggest that *A. afarensis* should replace *A. africanus* in this role" (White, Johanson, and Kimbel 1981, 467). As they observe in this 1981 paper written with their colleague Bill Kimbel, this is not the first time that the ancestral status of *Australopithecus africanus* had been challenged. "Tobias grappled with the Robinsonian dichotomy and concluded: ' . . . the two australopithecine taxa are very much more closely related than has commonly been averred hitherto.' . . . Later, Tobias even suggested that the holotype of *A. africanus* was actually a representative of *A. robustus*" (446). According to White and associates, the discoveries at Hadar and Laetoli lend new support to Tobias's claim: "The South African gracile australopithecine lacks elements in the suite of primitive characters described above for the Hadar and Laetoli hominids. It seems to share several distinctive, derived characters with later robust australopithecines" (1979, 327). In fact, White and associates conclude by proposing that the gracile australopithecines represent a link between the basal undifferentiated hominids at Hadar and Laetoli and the later robust australopithecines" (328). *Australopithecus africanus*, removed from its common ancestral slot, now plays a subordinate role: middle link between the robust australopithecines and the new common ancestor, *Australopithecus afarensis*.

Tobias and the Recovery of Australopithecus africanus

White and associates present this new view, once again, as a fulfillment of Tobias's claims: "Tobias emphasized the close relationship between *A. africanus* and *A. robustus* and prophetically postulated a yet-to-be-recognized, undifferentiated Pliocene *Australopithecus* species" (1981, 447). Yet, as Tobias makes clear in his 1980 response to Johanson and White, he was opposed to their interpretation of the Hadar and Laetoli finds. According to Tobias,

the fossils were too similar to *Australopithecus africanus* to warrant
a new species name: "In a word '*A. afarensis*' cannot be separated
from *A. africanus* on the characters that have been adduced" (1980,
9). In the same manner that Robinson challenged the existence of
Homo habilis as a separate form, so Tobias questions the reality of
"*Australopithecus afarensis.*" In contrast to his position in the debate
with Robinson, in which he maximized the distance between
Australopithecus africanus and *Homo*, he now emphasizes, as Robinson did, their affinity. In fact, he turns Robinson into an ally:
"The ultimate expression of the closeness of this relationship
[between *Australopithecus africanus* and *Homo*] was the submis-
sion of Robinson (1966, 1972) that the fossils assigned to *A.
africanus* should be taken out of the genus *Australopithecus* and
reclassified in the genus *Homo* as *Homo africanus*" (Tobias 1980,
2).

Tobias adopts his old adversary's point of view, yet he appears to
be critical of Johanson and White's recent shift of perspective.

By 1978 Johanson, Coppens and White . . . had accepted the
view that the hominids from the two sites belonged in the genus
Australopithecus and that they were close to, if not identical
with, the southern African taxon *A. africanus transvaalensis*. . . .

It is interesting to note that not long ago Johanson and Taieb
(1976) and Johanson et al. (1976) were so impressed with certain robust elements in the *Hadar* population as to have suggested the possible presence of "an early occurrence of a robust
australopithecine lineage." (1980, 5–13)

As for Tobias's own claims concerning the robust elements of
Australopithecus africanus: "On several occasions I have speculated
on the possible explanations for these robust-like elements in the
Makapansgat gracile australopithecines and most recently have in-
clined to the view that they are an expression of polymorphism in
A. africanus transvaalensis" (13).

Tobias finds support for his new view of *Australopithecus africanus* as a polymorphic or highly variable species in the discoveries
at Hadar and Laetoli:

On the view propounded here the place of *A. africanus* in time, space and phylogeny is confirmed and strengthened by the valuable new finds of Laetoli and Hadar. These early East African hominids have added greatly to the probability that *A. africanus* was a polytypic species, part of an evolving lineage of ancestral hominids from at least 3,7 to about 2,5 My B.P. These hominids occupied a late-Pliocene time-slot. . . . In this sense *A. africanus* from the Transvaal, Tanzania and Ethiopia is most likely to have been the common ancestor of both later lineages of hominids. (15)

Nevertheless, Tobias concedes that there may be points of difference between the Hadar remains and the South African fossils: "If further close morphological and statistical analysis confirms the presence of these small marks of distinction, it may be necessary to recognize and name a separate subspecies within the evolving and polytypic lineage *A. africanus*. . . . I propose *Australopithecus africanus aethiopicus* as a suitable name for this Ethiopian taxon" (14). Tobias had already proposed a new name for the remains from Laetoli: "At the same 1978 Nobel symposium at which Johanson formally announced the proposal to establish a new species, '*A. afarensis*', I suggested in my paper that the Laetoli hominids should be regarded as the Tanzanian subspecies of *A. africanus* under the nomen *A. africanus tanzaniensis*" (14).

Though they may disagree over the taxonomy of the Hadar and Laetoli remains, Johanson and Tobias are in accord in believing that these fossils have deeper significance. As Johanson observed in his 1983 speech to the American Humanists Association,

I do think very seriously that, for the millions of years that they have lain in sort of suspended animation in these beds, they have waited in a strange way to reveal to us something interesting about our beginnings. . . .

As we go back and look at some of our ancestors, we see the side branch of human evolution as a novel experience that culminated in a species capable of exploring and unravelling its own beginning. I think that the species today, *Homo sapiens*, is on the brink of the next evolutionary step. Millions of years ago, our ancestors stood on the brink of the savannah, on the edge of the forest, watching the forest disappear because of changes in the environment. Some of them ventured out into that new world and saw that new world in a different light from the world in which they had been evolving for millions of years. It stimulated them, it excited them, and eventually they adapted to it through this mechanism for culture that ultimately we call the mind. It was an experiment, it was a chance, that was susceptible to the whims and caprices of the natural world. Today we have moved so far away and so quickly from them that technologically we're here but biologically we're still back on the savannah grassland. (1983, 24)

Like the hero of Keith's account, man drags a paleolithic brain and body. Nature took a chance with man, as she did in Keith's tale, and now she may lose her gamble.

I am terribly worried about the future, because we have developed the ability to look after ourselves or not look after ourselves. If we can accept that we have common origins with Lucy and other fossils, it becomes extremely tantalizing to contemplate the idea that we have a common destiny. I think that, if we understand that we are at an important evolutionary juncture, that we are contemplating a new evolutionary step, and that the success or failure of this evolutionary step is really in our hands, and if we want our descendants to one day look back on their ancestry and ask where they came from, we've got to prevent someone from pushing the button. Because if it happens, it's over—there won't be anything to look back on. (24)

At first glance, Johanson's dim view reflects an old image of man:

> Created half to rise, and half to fall;
> Great lord of all things, yet prey to all;
> Sole judge of Truth, in endless error hurl'd;
> The glory, jest and riddle of the world.

Pope describes man "in *endless* error hurl'd"; he says nothing about man's annihilation. In fact, we live in a different universe from the one that Pope inhabited. Fate is "in our hands" instead of the hand of Providence. We have the ability "to look after ourselves *or not look after ourselves.*" Man's place in nature has changed even since Huxley's day. We stand under the shadow of a mushroom cloud rather than on the roseate Alps and Andes.

Epilogue
New Stories of
Human Evolution

I know no study which is so unutterably saddening as that of the evolution of humanity. . . . Out of the darkness of prehistoric ages man emerges
with the marks of his lowly origin strong upon him. He is a brute, only
more intelligent than the other brutes; a blind prey to impulses, which as
often as not lead him to destruction; a victim to endless illusions, which
make his mental existence a terror and a burden, and fill his physical life
with barren toil and battle. He attains a certain degree of physical com-
fort, and develops a more or less workable theory of life, in such favourable situations as the plains of Mesopotamia or of Egypt, and then, for
thousands and thousands of years, struggles with varying fortunes,
attended by infinite wickedness, bloodshed and misery.

—THOMAS HENRY HUXLEY (1889)

Though Huxley's optimism would wane toward the end of his life,
his faith in the grandeur of the study of human evolution was still
alive in his after-dinner rendering of the myth of science. This book
has told a different version of the myth, but in the same spirit. In
demonstrating that paleoanthropologists have been constrained by
the rules of art, my purpose has been to strengthen scientific theories of human evolution. I am committed to the belief that an awareness of narrative can benefit the study of human evolution. Given
that evolutionary explanation is by definition a kind of narration,
paleoanthropologists might consider wrestling with the "story-telling
dragon," rather than avoiding it altogether.

Some literary scholars would argue that there is no escape. It is
storytelling that makes us human (Forster 1927; Jameson 1981;
Ricoeur 1984). Even the impulse *not* to tell a story grows out of our

natural inclination to tell a tale. This is the impulse behind much modern fiction (Caserio 1979). Though it requires great literary skill to subvert narrative form, novelists are not the only ones to make the attempt. Historians and other scholars have tried to resist narrative procedure. This is also the impulse behind recent scholarship in the social sciences. According to the philosopher Jean-Francois Lyotard, the hallmark of contemporary "postmodern" culture is the disappearance of the grand narrative as a credible form of knowledge. Others such as Fredric Jameson "posit, not the disappearance of the great master-narratives but their passage underground, as it were, their continuing but now *unconscious* effectivity as a way of 'thinking about' and acting in our current situation" (Lyotard 1984, xii). According to Jameson, the persistence of "buried master-narratives" in non-Western and Western expressive forms merely "reconfirms the status of storytelling as the supreme function of the human mind." (1981, 123). Though they may not go quite this far, scientists have acknowledged that storytelling may have a biological basis. Some have suggested that mythmaking serves to counteract, or at the least warn us of, our innate aggressiveness and self-destructiveness. The ability to tell stories has adaptive value and thus could have evolved in humans as a species-specific characteristic (Cartmill 1983).[1]

"Can we comprehend myth in its biological functions," the philosopher Leszek Kolakowski asks in *The Presence of Myth*, "and also comprehend our own biology mythologically?" (1989, 114). The fact of the universal presence of myth has begun to be incorporated into biological theories, but the other question remains: can we comprehend our own biology mythologically? This question can be rephrased: is narrative a tool for understanding human evolution? How, exactly, can an awareness of narrative benefit paleoanthropology? Philosophers such as T. A. Goudge, Carl Hempel, and David Hull have discussed the narrative aspects of science, but few scien-

---

1. In *The Remembered Present* (1989), the biologist Gerald Edelman observes that the hallmark of human consciousness is the ability to draw conceptual links between present, future and past, though he does not draw an explicit connection to narrative.

tists have examined their own theories as narratives. What is the use in reading paleoanthropological—or any scientific—writing in this manner? Paleoanthropology is the most intimate but it is not the only science to arise out of the grand narrative tradition. Cosmology, geology, and paleontology also seek to reconstruct histories of a single entity—the cosmos, the planet, a species—each of which may be the subject of a narrative. Even subatomic particles may be depicted as protagonists of their own adventure stories as revealed in the title of a recent book, *Deep Time: The Journey of a Single Subatomic Particle from the Moment of Creation to the Death of the Universe and Beyond* (Darling 1989). So too the theories of the social sciences—psychology, sociology, economics, cultural anthropology—may have their heroes and donors.

One use of a narrative approach such as the one taken here is to analyze contemporary scientific theories for the purpose of achieving intersubjective agreement. One of the central messages of this book is that early-twentieth-century paleoanthropologists inhabited different conceptual worlds, governed by different causal principles. The debate over Piltdown hid even deeper differences of belief about the evolutionary forces which rule the planet. Though contemporary scientists may not hold beliefs as disparate as Keith and Elliot Smith, still they may inhabit different conceptual worlds, depending on their background and interests. They may speak different languages that they assume are the same, using similar words to encode quite different scientific conceptions. These subjective differences, in particular differences about causal mechanism, might be clarified by identifying the donor figures of these scientific theories. Scientists might consciously represent their theories as narratives (not necessarily according to the scheme used here) to find out areas of agreement and disagreement.

Postulating an underlying narrative structure may be a way of clarifying ambiguous points and also of uncovering deeper differences. In this regard, a narrative approach has much in common with the games approach of Sherwood Washburn. According to Washburn's approach, each scientist must specify the rules by which he or she normally "plays," for "the evolution game played with molecular information, immunochemistry, functional anatomy, and behavior is a very different game than one which is limited to fossils" (1973, 68). As Washburn observes, "The point of regarding the study of evolution as a game is to keep possibilities open, to play with many kinds of evidence, and to avoid the illusion that there is so much information that very definite final conclusions are possible" (69).

This brings us to a second use for a narrative approach: to create new hypotheses. The other central message of this book is that paleoanthropologists have told the same story over and over. This story, first recounted in the days when fossils were few, has constrained the interpretation of new fossil discoveries. It is by *constraining* interpretations of new fossil finds that narrative has held paleoanthropology captive. Perhaps the most important of these interpretations emerges not from any individual find—the famous Lucy skeleton or the ER 1470 skull or the newly discovered "black skull" (WT 17000)—but instead from the total array of fossils. At least seven kinds of hominid have been identified between 3.5 and 1 million years ago in Africa (Delson 1986). From this perspective, the fossil record may appear to support the notion that we are truly heroes to have survived. Or it can tell a different story: we are merely the remnants of a golden age, the "last gasp of a richer ancestry" (Gould 1989, 35). Whichever meaning is chosen, it has been clear to paleoanthropologists for some time that the course of human evolution is not a single linear sequence leading inexorably to man, with an occasional detour leading to a dead-end form such as *Australopithecus robustus* or Neanderthal. Nor can it be represented as a pair of diverging lines—hominized versus less hominized, ancestral versus nonancestral—defined in terms of their relationship to modern humans. The recent discovery of a 2.5-million-year-old hyperrobust australopithecine cranium, dubbed the "black skull" for its darkly mineralized bone, suggests that the australopithecines themselves may occupy at least three lineages, each following its own evolutionary pathway.

New fossil discoveries have sent paleoanthropologists back to the phylogenetic drawing board, and yet an even more difficult task awaits: how do we render these new images into words? How do we turn these complicated phylogenies, with their perplexing and intricate network of intersecting, diverging, and parallel paths, into stories? Taking into account the provisional nature of these phylogenies and also their diversity, we might reframe this last question: how do we render into narrative form not just the network of phylogenetic paths but also alternative *possible* networks?

In the short story "The Garden of Forking Paths," the writer Jorge Luis Borges compares the writing of a story to the construction of a labyrinth. The labyrinth is itself an attempt to render "the web of time—the strands of which approach one another, bifurcate, intersect or ignore each other through the centuries—embracing *every* possibility. We do not exist in most of them. In some you exist and not I, while in others I do, and you do not, and in yet others both of us exist" (1962, 100). Whether or not it is agreed that time itself consists of a web of bifurcating and intersecting strands, Borges's conception of a labyrinth is suggestive. For the purposes of telling the story of *how* humans have come to exist, paleoanthropologists might view their branching phylogenies as a "garden of forking paths." Here a series of questions would be asked: Who were the first hominids? When and where did they come to the ground and why? The more detailed the question, the more revealing the story. According to Borges's procedure, "all the possible solutions occur, each one being the point of departure for other bifurcations" (98). The goal would be to reconstruct not a single evolutionary pathway or even multiple paths but the full set of *possible* arrangements. Following Borges a further step, we might imagine circumstances under which australopithecines evolve but not humans, or humans but not australopithecines, as a way of gaining a perspective on how both of them actually did come into existence.

In *Wonderful Life*, Stephen Jay Gould conducts a similar thought-experiment. Imagining himself to be a "divine disc jockey," Gould predicts what would happen if we coul. 'replay life's tape":

Any replay of the tape would leaa evolution down a pathway radically different from the road actually taken. But the conse-

quent differences in outcome do not imply that evolution is sense-
less, and without meaningful pattern. But the diversity of possible itineraries does demonstrate that eventual results cannot be
predicted at the outset. Each step proceeds for cause, but no
finale can be specified at the start, and none would ever occur a
second time in the same way, because any pathway proceeds
through thousands of improbable stages. (1989, 51)

The purpose in replaying life's tape is to replace old teleological
habits of thought with a new perspective. Gould is a prophet of a
"different view of life": the control by immediate events over destiny
(284). Gould evokes the new divinity:

Its name is contingency—and contingency is a thing unto itself,
not the titration of determinism by randomness. Science has been
slow to admit the different explanatory world of history into its
domain—and our interpretations have been impoverished by this
omission. Science has also tended to denigrate history, when
forced to a confrontation, by regarding any invocation of contingency as less elegant or less meaningful than explanations
based directly on timeless "laws of nature." (51)

Yet the principle of contingency has had eminent scientific adherents. Darwin himself recognized the importance of timing and
order in the sequence of events. As we have seen in *The Descent of
Man*, natural selection is "summoned" by the sequence of events
rather than "commanding" those events to happen. Darwin also
recognized "the central distinction between *laws in the background*
and *contingency in the details*" (290): that general principles "set
the channels in which organic design must evolve" but that the
details—the specific set of circumstances and events which lead to
the evolution of a human instead of a chimp—lie in the realm of
contingency.

This is a useful lesson. But paleoanthropologists want to know
how human evolution *did* occur, after all. How might we tell the
story of human evolution as though we did not know where it would
go and yet end up, all the same, with humans? An answer may lie in

William James's essay "The Dilemma of Determinism." There he suggests how one might reconcile a belief in indeterminism—of a universe in which the parts have a certain amount of "loose play" so that the laying down of one does not necessarily determine what the others shall be—with a belief in a world governed by a creator. (James's aim was not to demonstrate that such a creator exists but to make the idea of indeterminism less offensive to those who believed in one. For our purposes, James's creator might fill the same role as Gould's divine disc jockey or Borges's novelist.)

> If you allow him to provide possibilities as well as actualities to the universe, and to carry on his own thinking in those two categories just as we do ours, chances may be there, uncontrolled even by him, and the course of the universe be really ambiguous; and yet the end of all things may be just what he intended it to be from all eternity. . . .
>
> The creator's plan of the universe would thus be left blank as to many of its actual details, but all possibilities would be marked down. The realization of some of these would be left absolutely to chance; that is, would only be determined when the moment of realization came. Other possibilities would be *contingently* determined; that is, their decision would have to wait till it was seen how the matters of absolute chance fell out. But the rest of the plan, including its final upshot, would be rigorously determined once for all. So the creator himself would not need to know *all* the details of actuality until they came; and at any time his own view of the world would be a view partly of facts and partly of possibilities. (1897, 180–82)

James draws the critical distinction between contingency and chance and also the crucial implication.

> The great point is that the possibilities are really *here*. Whether it be we who solve them, or he working through us, at those soul-trying moments when fate's scales seem to quiver . . . is of small account, so long as we admit that the issue is decided nowhere else than *here* and *now*. *That* is what gives the palpitating

reality to our moral life and makes it tingle . . . with so strange and elaborate an excitement. This reality, this excitement, are what the determinisms, hard and soft alike, suppress by their denial that *anything* is decided here and now, and their dogma that all things were foredoomed and settled long ago. (183)

James's passage stands in striking contrast to Huxley's epigraph with its gloomy view of man, trudging from the darkness of the prehistoric past into the darkness of the predetermined future, despite all his "workable theories."

This brings us to an important question: Why tell stories of human evolution? Can an awareness of narrative benefit society? Can stories of human evolution provide a guide for human conduct in the present and the future? Can they provide "a workable theory of life," as well as a workable theory of science? As the paleoanthropologist Matt Cartmill observes,

> People who study human origins sometimes claim that their investigations will shed new light on human nature and so help us to understand ourselves and predict the future. But this is wishful thinking. A thing is what it is, no matter how it got to be that way; and human appetites and impulses are what they are, no matter where or what we came from. Knowing their history adds nothing. If it were proved tomorrow that people evolved from cottontails instead of apes, we would still prefer bananas to clover as an ingredient in pie. (1983, 65).

Yet some human preferences do change: if clover were to become fashionable we might eat it in salad instead of fiddleheads or arugula. Our beliefs and customs do affect the way we behave. "Intelligence, at least of the human sort, involves making internal models of the world and acting on them," Cartmill himself observes.

> Granting this, our myths are grounds for optimism. For well over a century, the artists and writers of scientifically advanced countries have poured forth a steady stream of symbols, images, and stories calling for vigilance against the time when planetary suicide would be within our grasp. Bolstered by scientific specu-

lation, these mythic images have assumed the form of a half-perceived religious vision, believed in by millions and communicated by every medium available. The fact that our story-tellers taught us such fear is a heartening mystery. Some of them are now beginning to tell new origin stories that counsel us to courage and optimism instead of fear. When we evaluate the new stories, we need to pay attention not only to their fidelity to the facts but also to their implications about what it means to be human—because the place that we claim for ourselves in our internal models of the universe may help determine whether we are ultimately to have any place in it at all. (78)

In the final analysis, the *truly* significant test of scientific theories of human evolution may lie in their workability in everyday practice.

This is the essence of the pragmatic approach of William James. For James, the final test of truth rests not with humanity as a whole but with each individual.

This personal method of appeal seems to be among the very conditions of the problem; and the most one can do is to confess as candidly as he can the grounds for the faith that is in him, and leave his example to work on others as it may.

Let me, then, without circumlocution say just this. The world is enigmatical enough in all conscience, whatever theory we may take up toward it. The indeterminism I defend . . . represents that world as vulnerable, and liable to be injured by certain of its parts if they act wrong. And it represents their acting wrong as a matter of possibility or accident, neither inevitable nor yet to be infallibly warded off. . . . It gives us a pluralistic, restless universe, in which no single point of view can ever take in the whole scene. (1897, 176−77).

Not even, I would venture, the Saturnian perspective. Though we are very closely related to the living apes, as Huxley showed, we are also quite different. Though we easily learn to cooperate with members of our own group, as Darwin observed, we easily learn to kill those we identify as other. Accepting this, we each have a choice: we can choose to cooperate by identifying ourselves as members of ever-larger groups.[2] I earlier suggested that we trace the separate hominid lineages down their divergent and intersecting paths, but we might also consider broadening the "us unit" to include all hominid species—not to mention, women, children, and those human groups who have been largely left out of Western accounts[3]—as part of the same family story. We might tell the common story not just of all hominids but of all hominoids, and even of all mammals. Some paleoanthropologists have chosen this route for scientific reasons: viewing humans *as hominoids* or *as mammals* has been a fruitful research strategy. For the purposes of constructing workable theories of life, we might extend our affinity even further—to the Brazilian rain forests and even to inanimate things such as the ozone layer—by identifying ourselves as members of the same planet. We might tell stories in which not just the sequence of events but also the characters manifest "a deeper kind of belonging."

Just as books on human evolution typically begin by recounting the famous Oxford debate, they often close by reminding us of the risks of forgetting our unity with the rest of nature. In the end, my point is not to tell a new story of human evolution but to advocate the telling of such narratives, both scientific and popular. This may appear a contradiction: scientific theories of human evolution have suffered from obeying the laws of popular art, in particular from viewing our evolution as a hero story. Yet, as I have just suggested, if we were really to stop looking for our own self-image in the world then the stories that we tell would be that much less poetically rich, that much less engaging to a wider audience. The obvious solution

2. Even sociobiologists such as Richard Dawkins who emphasize the "ruthless selfishness of the gene," allow humans the chance—though limited—to shape their own destiny. "Let us try to *teach* generosity and altruism, because we are born selfish. Let us understand what our own selfish genes are up to, because we may then at least have the chance to upset their designs, something which no other species has ever aspired to" (1976, 3).

3. One of the major limitations of the present work is its neglect of the themes of gender and race in theories of human origins. See Haraway (1989), Tanner and Zihlman (1976), Zihlman (1978, 1987), Fedigan (1986), and Fee (1982) for a discussion of—and alternatives to—male-centered theories of human evolution.

is to recognize that even popular accounts need not follow the hero-centered linear conceptions of folktale and myth. Still, we may wonder, should scientists tell these more popular stories? Or should they merely provide the raw material for more poetic conceptions? There is another possibility. In their book *Anthropology as Cultural Critique* (1986), Marcus and Fischer "understand ethnography, in its experimental transformation and critical possibilities, to be a disciplined vehicle for empirical research and writing that explore the same sorts of debates that concern Western art and philosophy" (167–68). Should paleoanthropology be a form of cultural criticism?

The answer, I think, rests with the individual paleoanthropologist. It was my training as a paleoanthropologist that led me to see the relevance of a narrative approach, but it was a feeling for the story and for the bigger question—why are we here?—that drew me to study human evolution in the first place. Not all paleoanthropologists are engaged by the narrative aspect of the field. Nor have they necessarily been drawn in by the desire to answer the question: how did we become human? Storytelling is only one aspect of what most paleoanthropologists do (though I would argue that it pervades other activities, such as the description of fossils). Nor is it necessarily the most imaginative aspect. Paleoanthropologists have displayed great ingenuity in devising methods to formulate and test propositions about human evolution. But it is also true that if paleoanthropologists were limited to asserting the explicit propositions they could prove, human evolution would in the end be unthinkable. As Paul Ricoeur has observed, history begins in an attempt to redeem our sense of "being in time" by advancing hypotheses about the connections among different human states of affairs which we can never know for certain but which, being human, we all care about. The same may be said of paleoanthropology. It may also be said that therein lies the grandeur of the study. Perhaps we should teach students how to tell stories, just as we show them how to measure bones and teeth. To tell *new* stories will require skill, as well as enthusiasm and imagination.

Bibliography

Anonymous, 1927. "Man and his ancestry," *Nature* 120:321–24.

Ayala, F. J. 1977. "'Nothing in biology makes sense except in the light of evolution': Theodosius Dobzhansky, 1900–1975," *J. Hered.* 68:3–10.

Ayala, F. J., and T. Dobzhansky, eds. 1974. *Studies in the Philosophy of Biology* (University of California Press, Berkeley and Los Angeles).

Bal, M. 1985. *Introduction to the Theory of Narrative* (University of Toronto Press, Toronto).

Barthes, R. 1977. "Introduction to the Structural Analysis of Myth," in *Image Music Text* (Hill and Wang, New York).

Beer, G. 1983. *Darwin's Plots: Evolutionary Narrative in Darwin, George Eliot and Nineteenth-Century Fiction* (Routledge and Kegan Paul, London).

Bettelheim, B. 1977. *The Uses of Enchantment* (Vintage, New York).

Borges, J. L. 1962. "The Garden of Forking Paths," in *Ficciones* (Grove, New York), 89–101.

Bowler, P. J. 1986. *Theories of Human Evolution: A Century of Debate, 1844–1944* (Johns Hopkins University Press, Baltimore).

Cartmill, M. 1983. "Four legs good, two legs bad," *Nat. Hist.* 11:65–78.

Caserio, R. 1979. *Plot, Story and the Novel* (Princeton University Press, Princeton).

Cave, A. J. E. 1937. "A master anatomist," in *Sir Grafton Elliot Smith: A Biographical Record by His Colleagues,* ed. W. R. Dawson (Jonathan Cape, London), 185–202.

Clifford, J. 1988. *The Predicament of Culture* (Harvard University Press, Cambridge).

Culler, J. 1975. *Structuralist Poetics* (Cornell University Press, Ithaca, New York).

Darling, D. 1989. *Deep Time: The Journey of a Single Subatomic Particle from the Moment of Creation to the Death of the Universe and Beyond* (Delacorte, New York).

Dart, R. 1925. "*Australopithecus africanus*: the man-ape of south Africa," *Nature* 115:195–99.

———. 1926. "Taungs and its significance," *Nat. Hist.* 26:315–30.

———. 1953. "The predatory transition from ape to man," *Int. Anthrop. & Ling. Rev.* 1 (4):201–18.

———. 1955. "Cultural status of the south African man-apes," *Ann. Rept. Smiths. Instit.*, 317–38.

Darwin, C. 1948. *The Origin of Species* [1859] *and The Descent of Man* [1871] (Modern Library, New York).

Dawkins, R. 1976. *The Selfish Gene* (Oxford University Press, London).

Dawson, W. R. 1938. *Sir Grafton Elliot Smith: A Biographical Record by His Colleagues* (Jonathan Cape, London).

Delson, E. 1986. "Human phylogeny revised again," *Nature* 322: 496–97.

Dobzhansky, T. 1937. *Genetics and the Origin of Species* (Columbia University Press, New York).

———. 1961. "Man and natural selection," *Amer. Sci.* 49:285–99.

———. 1963. *Mankind Evolving* (Yale University Press, New Haven).

Edelman, G. E. 1989. *The Remembered Present* (Basic Books, New York).

Elliot Smith, G. E. 1903. "On the morphology of the brain in the Mammalia with special reference to that of the Lemurs, recent and extinct," *Trans. Linn. Soc.* 8:319–432.

———. 1911. "Fossil remains of man," *Nature* 85:402–03.

———. 1912. "The evolution of man," *Rept. Brit. Assoc. Adv. Sci.*, 578–98.

———. 1913a. "The controversies concerning the interpretation and meaning of the remains of the Dawn-man found near Piltdown," *Proc. Manch. Lit. & Phil Soc.* (Nov.):vii–ix.

———. 1913b. "The Piltdown skull and brain cast," *Nature* 92: 318–19.

———. 1916. "Men of the Old Stone Age," *Amer. Mus. J.* 16:319–25.

———. 1922. "The brain of Piltdown man," *Nature* 109:355–56.

———. 1923. "The study of man," *Nature* 112:440–44.

———. 1924. *The Evolution of Man* (Oxford University Press, London).

———. 1925. "The question of race and hormones," *Nature* 116:855–56.

———. 1926. "Casts obtained from the brain cases of fossil men," *Nat. Hist.* 26:294–99.

———. 1927a. *Human Nature* (Watts, London).

———. 1927b. "The meaning of the brain," *Sci. Amer.* 136:13–16.

———. 1928a. *In the Beginning: The Origin of Civilization* (William Morrow, New York).

———. 1928b. "Neanderthal man not our ancestor," *Sci. Amer.* (August):112–15.

———. 1929. *Human History* (W. W. Norton, New York).

Fedigan, L. M. 1986. "The changing role of women in models of human evolution," *Ann. Rev. Anthrop.* 15:25–66.

Fee, E. 1982. "Woman's role in the evolution of humankind," *Sci. & Nat.* 5:20–29.

Forster, E. M. 1927. *Aspects of the Novel* (Harcourt Brace Jovanovich, New York).

Frye, N. 1957. *Anatomy of Criticism* (Princeton University Press, Princeton).

————. 1976. *The Secular Scripture* (Harvard University Press, Cambridge).

Goodman, N. 1978. *Ways of Worldmaking* (Hackett, Indianapolis).

Goudge, T. A. 1961. *The Ascent of Life* (University of Toronto Press, Toronto).

Gould, S. J. 1977. *Ever since Darwin: Reflections in Natural History* (W. W. Norton, New York).

————. 1989. *Wonderful Life* (W. W. Norton, New York).

Gregory, W. K. 1927. "The origin of man from the anthropoid stem —when and where?" *Proc. Amer. Philos. Soc.* 66:339—76.

————. 1934. *Man's Place among the Anthropoids: Three Lectures on the Evolution of Man from the Lower Vertebrates* (Clarendon Press, Oxford).

Greimas, J. 1970. *Du Sens* (Seuil, Paris).

Haeckel, E. H. 1868. *The History of Creation* (D. Appleton, New York).

————. 1897. *The Evolution of Man*, vols. 1 and 2 (D. Appleton, New York).

————. 1898. "On our recent knowledge of the origin of man," *Ann. Rept. Smiths. Instit.*, 461—80.

Haraway, D. 1989. *Primate Visions: Gender, Race, and Nature in the World of Modern Science* (Routledge, New York).

Hempel, C. 1966. *Philosophy of Natural Science* (Prentice-Hall, Englewood Cliffs, N.J.).

Hull, D. 1974. *Philosophy of Biological Science* (Prentice-Hall, Englewood Cliffs, N.J.).

Hutchinson, G. E. 1962. *The Enchanted Voyage and Other Studies* (Yale University Press, New Haven).

Huxley, L. 1901. *The Life and Letters of Thomas Henry Huxley* (D. Appleton, New York).

Huxley, T. H. 1863. *Man's Place in Nature* (University of Michigan Press, Ann Arbor, 1959).

————. 1883. "Science and Art," in *The World's Great Speeches*, ed. L. Copeland and L. W. Lamm (Dover, New York, 1973), 682—83.

————. 1889. "Agnosticism," *The Nineteenth Century* 25 (144): 170—94.

———. 1894. "Evolution and Ethics, Prolegomena," in *Evolution and Ethics and Other Essays* (Macmillan, London), 1–46.

Irvine, W. 1955. *Apes, Angels and Victorians* (McGraw-Hill, New York).

Isaac, G. 1982. *Early Stages in the Evolution of Human Behavior: The Adaptive Significance of Stone Tools* (University of Amsterdam, Amsterdam).

James, W. 1897. "The Dilemma of Determinism," in *The Will to Believe and Other Essays in Popular Philosophy* (Dover, New York, 1956) 145–83.

Jameson, F. 1972. *The Prison-House of Language* (Princeton University Press, Princeton).

———. 1981. *The Political Unconscious* (Cornell University Press, Ithaca, N.Y.).

Johanson, D. C. 1983. "The human career," *Humanist*, July/August, 22–24.

Johanson, D. C., and T. D. White. 1979. "A systematic assessment of early african hominids," *Science* 202:321–30.

Keith, A. 1894a. "The ligaments of the catarrhine monkeys with references to corresponding structures in man," *J. Anat. & Physiol.* 28:149–68.

———. 1894b. "Notes on a theory to account for the various arrangements of the flexor profundus digitorium in the hand and foot of the primates," *J. Anat. & Physiol.* 28:335.

———. 1895a. "Growth of brain in men and monkey, with a short criticism of the usual method of starting brain-ratios," *J. Anat. & Physiol.* 29:282–303.

———. 1895b. "The modes of origin of the carotid and subclavian arteries from the arch of the aorta in some of the higher primates," *J. Anat. & Physiol.* 29:453–58.

———. 1895c. "*Pithecanthropus erectus*—a brief review of human fossil remains," *Sc. Prog.* 3:348–69.

———. 1903. "The extent to which the posterior segments of the body have been transmuted and suppressed in the evolution of man and allied primates," *J. Anat. & Physiol.* 37:18–40.

————. 1911. *Ancient Types of Man* (Harper & Brothers, London and New York).

————. 1912. "Certain phases in the evolution of man: Part 1," *Brit. Med. J.* 1:734–37.

————. 1915. *The Antiquity of Man* (Williams & Norgate, London).

————. 1917. "Review of *Men of the Old Stone Age*," *Man* 17:82–85.

————. 1919. "The differentiation of mankind into racial types," *Nature* 112:301–05.

————. 1923a. "The adaptational machinery concerned in the evolution of the human body," *Nature* 112:257–68.

————. 1923b. "Man's posture: Its evolution and disorders," *Brit. Med. J.*, 1:451–54; 499–502; 545–48; 587–90; 624–26; 669–72.

————. 1925a. *The Antiquity of Man* (Williams & Norgate, London).

————. 1925b. "Concerning the rate of man's evolution," *Nature* 116:317–20.

————. 1925c. "Huxley as anthropologist," *Nature* 115:719–23.

————. 1925d. "The nature of man's structural imperfections," *Nature* 116:821–23; 867–69.

————. 1925e. "The new missing link," *Brit. Med. J.* 1:325–26.

————. 1925f. *The Religion of a Darwinist* (Watts, London).

————. 1926. "The gorilla and man as contrasted forms," *Lancet* 1:490–92.

————. 1927. "Darwin's theory of man's descent as it stands today," *Science* 66:201–08.

————. 1928. "The evolution of the human races," *J. Roy. Anthrop. Instit.* 58:305–21.

————. 1929. "Fossil man from Peking," *Lancet* 2:683.

————. 1930. "Recent discoveries of fossil man," *Nature* 125:935–42.

————. 1931. *New Discoveries Relating to the Antiquity of Man* (Williams & Norgate, London).

————. 1946. *Essays on Human Evolution* (Watts, London).

————. 1949. *A New Theory of Human Evolution* (Philosophical Library, New York).

————. 1950. *An Autobiography* (Watts, London).

Kolakowski, L. 1989. *The Presence of Myth* (University of Chicago Press, Chicago).

Kuhn, T. S. 1970. *The Structure of Scientific Revolutions* (University of Chicago Press, Chicago).

Landau, M. 1981. *The Anthropogenic: Paleoanthropological Writing as a Genre of Literature*, Ph.D. dissertation, Yale University.

————. 1984. "Human evolution as narrative," *Amer. Sci.* 72: 262–67.

————. 1986. "The Baron in the Trees," in *Proceedings International Meetings on Variability and Behavioral Evolution* (Academei dei Lincei, Rome), 263–74.

————. 1987. "Paradise Lost: The Theme of Terrestriality in Human Evolution," in *The Rhetoric of the Human Sciences*, ed. J. S. Nelson, A. Megill, D. N. McCloskey (University of Wisconsin Press, Madison), 111–24.

Lévi-Strauss, C. 1973. "La structure et la forme," in *Anthropologie Structurale*, vol. 2 (Plon, Paris), 139–73.

Lovejoy, A. O. 1936. *The Great Chain of Being* (Harvard University Press, Cambridge).

Lyotard, J.-F. 1984. *The Postmodern Condition: A Report on Knowledge* (University of Minnesota Press, Minneapolis).

MacKenzie, N. and J. 1973. *H. G. Wells* (Simon & Schuster, New York).

Marcus, G., and M. Fischer. 1986. *Anthropology as Cultural Critique* (University of Chicago Press, Chicago).

Millar, R. 1972. *The Piltdown Men* (Ballantine, New York).

Osborn, H. F. 1916. *Men of the Old Stone Age* (Scribner's, New York).

————. 1928. *Man Rises to Parnassus* (Princeton University Press, Princeton).

Owen, R. 1857. "On the characters, principles of division, and primary groups of the class Mammalia," *J. Proc. Linn. Soc.* 2: 1–45.

Pilbeam, D. 1972. *The Ascent of Man* (Macmillan, New York).

Propp, V. 1928. *Morphology of the Folktale* (University of Texas Press, Austin; English translation 1968).

Ricoeur, P. 1984. *Time and Narrative* (University of Chicago Press, Chicago).

Robinson, J. T. 1956. "An early chapter in the history of man," *S. Afr. Mus. Assoc. Bull.* 6:166–76.

———. 1961a. "The australopithecines and their bearing on the origin of man and stone tool-making," *S. Afr. J. Sci.* 57:3–13.

———. 1961b. "Australopithecines and the origin of man," *Ann. Rept. Smiths. Instit.*, 479–500.

———. 1965. "*Homo 'habilis'* and the australopithecines," *Nature*, 205:1–10.

Scholes, R. 1974. *Structuralism in Literature: An Introduction* (Yale University Press, New Haven).

Scholes, R., and R. Kellogg. 1966. *The Nature of Narrative* (Oxford University Press, London).

Sober, E., ed. 1984. *Conceptual Issues in Evolutionary Biology* (MIT Press, Cambridge).

Tanner, A., and A. Zihlman, 1976. Women in evolution (Part 1): Innovation and selection in human origins, *Signs* 1:585–608.

Tobias, P. V. 1965a. "Australopithecus, Homo habilis, tool-using and tool-making," *S. Afr. Arch. Bull.* 20:167–92.

———. 1965b. "Early man in east Africa," *Science* 149:22–33.

———. 1969. *Man's Past and Future* (Witwatersrand University Press, Johannesburg).

———. 1980. "'*Australopithecus afarensis*' and *A. africanus*: Critique and an alternative hypothesis," *Palaeont. Afr.* 23:1–17.

Todorov, T. 1981. *Introduction to Poetics* (University of Minnesota Press, Minnesota).

Washburn, S. L. 1973. "Human evolution: Science or game?" *Yrbk. Phys. Anth.* 17:67–70.

White, T. D., D. C. Johanson, and W. H. Kimbel. 1981. "*Australopithecus africanus*: Its phyletic position reconsidered," *S. Afr. J. Sci.* 77:445–70.

Williams G. C. 1966. *Adaptation and Natural Selection* (Princeton University Press, Princeton).

Wood Jones, F. 1916. *Arboreal Man* (Edward Arnold, London).

———. 1937. "In Egypt and Nubia," in *Sir Grafton Elliot Smith: A Biographical Sketch by His Colleagues*, ed. W. R. Dawson (Jonathan Cape, London), 139–49.

Zihlman, A. 1978. Women and evolution (Part 2): Subsistence and social organization among early hominids, *Signs* 4:4–20.

———. 1987. "Sex, sexes and sexism in human origins," *Yrbk. Phys. Anth.* 30:11–19.

Index